1st ADDITION.   7.50

FOUNDATIONS OF PRACTICAL MAGIC

Israel Regardie has long been one of the
leading authorities on the theory and
practice of magic. This collection of
essays brings together a lifetime's
experience of occult techniques to form
an accessible system of
practical magic.

By the same author

A GARDEN OF POMEGRANATES
HOW TO MAKE AND USE TALISMANS
PRACTICAL GUIDE TO GEOMANTIC DIVINATION
ROLL AWAY THE STONE
THE EYE IN THE TRIANGLE
THE GOLDEN DAWN
THE MIDDLE PILLAR
THE PHILOSOPHER'S STONE
THE TREE OF LIFE
TWELVE STEPS TO SPIRITUAL ENLIGHTENMENT

FOUNDATIONS OF PRACTICAL MAGIC

An Introduction to Qabalistic, Magical and Meditative Techniques

by

ISRAEL REGARDIE

THE AQUARIAN PRESS LIMITED
Wellingborough, Northamptonshire

First published 1979

ISBN 0 85030 197 1

Photoset by Specialised Offset Services Ltd, Liverpool.
Printed by Biddles Ltd., Guildford, Surrey
and bound by Redwood Burn Ltd., Esher.

CONTENTS

1. THE ART AND MEANING OF MAGIC

1. Magic in East and West

When I was about seventeen years of age, a friend loaned me a copy of Major L.A. Waddell's *Lamaism*. In those days it impressed me tremendously, no doubt because of its massive size. In every sense it was a heavy tome, and tomes then suggested depth and weight of scholarship and insight. Naturally I knew nothing at that time about Magic, and beyond a few theosophical allusions next to nothing of Buddhism. So the greater part of the significance and wide erudition of the book must have passed me by completely, though it is a veritable storehouse of knowledge.

Then, out of the blue it reappeared on my horizon, again, through the agency of a friend. In the light of the little knowledge and experience gained through the passage of several years, its contents excited me enormously — and it was with the utmost interest that I reconsidered it. For me, one of the things that stood out most emphatically this time was the extraordinary similarity between — even the fundamental unity of — the highest and most basic magical conceptions of both East and West. Whether this is due, as many exponents of the Eastern wisdom would claim, to the direct importation of occult philosophy and practice from the Orient to western civilization, it is not my intention now to argue. Nonetheless, it is my considered belief that in occidental countries there has definitely been a secret tradition on a practical level — a tradition which for centuries has orally transmitted the finer part of this magical knowledge. In fact, so jealously reserved at all times was this tradition that by most people it was hardly suspected at all. Very few were the fortunate individuals who in any age were drawn as though by invisible currents of spiritual affinity to the concealed portals of its temples.

Occasionally a small portion of this closely concealed tradition wormed its way outwards into books. Some of these latter are those which were written by Iamblichus and the later Neoplatonists, and also by students such as Cornelius Agrippa, Pietro d'Abano, and Eliphas Lévi, etc. Its cruder elements found expression in the far-famed Clavicles, Grimoires and Goetias. Yet for the most part the true sequence of teaching, and the vast implications of its practical knowledge were, as above stated, maintained in strict privacy. The reason for this secrecy may have been the feeling that there are only a small number in any age, in any country, amongst any people, who are likely to appreciate or understand the deeper or sublimer aspects of Theurgy, the higher magic. It requires sympathy, much insight and a capacity for hard work, which, needless to say, few people possess. And there is, consequently, but little point scattering broadcast these pearls of bright wisdom which can only be misunderstood.

Indubitably this conclusion is corroborated by Waddell's *Lamaism*. In point of fact, a good deal of so-called esoteric magical knowledge is there contained – though it is presented wholly without comprehension. Hence his statement of that particular aspect of Lamaism is vitiated and rendered practically worthless. And while I may agree with Waddell that some of the Lamaistic practices have little to do with historical Buddhism, his sneers as regards an esoteric Buddhism on the magical side of things are simply laughable, for his own book is a clear demonstration of precisely that one fact which he has perceived not at all.

His book, obviously, was intended primarily to be an objective account of the Buddhism indigenous to Tibet and as practised by its monks and hermits. Unfortunately, the prejudices and mis-understandings of the author are scarcely concealed. So that, while indubitably he did pick up some of the crumbs dropped haphazard from the esoteric table of the Lamas, and recorded them probably as he found them, nevertheless he had not the necessary training, knowledge or insight into the subject possessed undoubtedly by some of the higher initiated Lamas with whom he had conversed. The result was that he was unable to make anything of that information. In fact, *his* account of their practices sounds simply silly and absurd. Psychologically, he succeeds not in throwing ridicule on the Lamas but only upon himself.

Certain aspects of Theurgy or western Magic have now been comparatively clearly set forth. Some early reviewers and critics were of the opinion that my former work *The Tree of Life* was as plain an elementary statement of its major traditional principles as had yet publicly been made. And Dion Fortune's book *The Mystical Qabalah*, a frank masterpiece, is likewise an incomparably fine rendition of the mystical philosophy that underlies the practice of Magic. I therefore suggest that by employing the theorems laid down in those two books, and applying them to the material in Waddell's *Lamaism*, we may arrive at an understanding of some otherwise obscure portions of Tibetan Magic.

Primal Concerns of Magic

It may be well, at first, to confess that a good part of the magical routine refers to a psychic plane, to certain levels of the collective unconscious, though by no means does that wholly condemn it as certain mystical schools feel inclined to do. Other branches concern such phenomenal accomplishments as rain-making, obtaining good crops, scaring away demons, and similar feats with which both eastern and occidental legend have familiarized us – feats, moreover, which require a good deal of explaining away by the rationalist and mechanistic scientist. Finally, there is that unhappily large part which verges on witchcraft pure and simple. With this latter, I am at no time concerned.

But I maintain, as a primal definition, that Magic, whether of the eastern or western variety, is essentially a divine process – Theurgy, a mode of spiritual culture or development. From the psychological viewpoint, it may be interpreted as a series of techniques having as their object the withdrawal of energy from objective and subjective objects so that, in the renewal of consciousness by a re-emergent libido, the jewel of a transformed life with new creative possibilities and with spontaneity may be found. It comprises various technical methods, some simple in nature, others highly complex and most difficult to perform, for purifying the personality, and into that cleansed organism, freed of pathogenic strain, invoking the higher self.

With this in mind, then, a good many of the apparently unrelated items of Magic, some of its invocations and visualizing practices, take on a new and added significance. They are important psychological steps whereby to repair, improve or elevate consciousness so that eventually it may prove a worthy vehicle of the Divine Light. A sentence or two written many years ago by William Quan Judge in his pamphlet *An Epitome of Theosophy* express so exactly the impression to be conveyed that it is convenient to quote: 'The real object to be kept in view is to so open up or make porous the lower nature that the spiritual nature may shine through it and become the guide and ruler.

It is only "cultivated" in the sense of having a vehicle prepared for its use, into which it may descend.'

This conception is likewise the point of view of our magical system. The technical forms of Magic described in *The Golden Dawn*, such as Pentagram and other rituals, astral assumption of God-forms, evocations (though not necessarily to physical manifestation) of elemental and planetary spirits, skrying in the spirit-vision, and the invocation of the Holy Guardian Angel, are all performed with that single objective held ever before one. Theurgy and the exponents of the Eastern mysticisms are thus in complete accord on the fundamental theoretical principles.

Objective Misconceptions

To illustrate now what I mean by the complete misunderstanding which a purely objective account of magical practices is capable of achieving, it will be found interesting to consider but a few statements made by Waddell. First of all, let me quote from page 152 (2nd edition) of his work: 'The purest Ge-lug-pa Lama on awaking every morning, and before venturing outside his room, fortifies himself against assault by the demons by first of all assuming the spiritual guise of his fearful tutelary ... Thus when the Lama emerges from his room ... he presents spiritually the appearance of the demon-king, and the smaller malignant demons, being deluded into the belief that the Lama is indeed their own vindictive king, they flee from his presence, leaving the Lama unharmed.'

Surely this is a puerile interpretation. Though the fact itself of the assumption of the spiritual forms of tutelary deities is perfectly correct, the rationale he provides is infantile and stupid. So far as western Theurgy is concerned, centuries of effort have shown that one of the most potent adjuncts to spiritual experience, as aiding the assimilation of the lower self into the all-inclusive psyche, is the astral assumption of the magical form of a divine force or a god. By means of an exaltation of the mind and soul to its presence, whilst giving utterance to an invocation, it is conceded that there may be a descent of the Light into the heart of the devotee, accompanied *pari passu* by an ascent of the mind towards the ineffable splendour of the spirit.

God-forms

So far as the reason for and explanation of this process is concerned, it may be well to state briefly that according to the magical hypothesis, the whole cosmos is permeated and vitalized by one omnipresent Life, which in itself is both immanent as well as transcendent. At the dawn of the manifestation of the universe from the thrice unknown darkness, there issue forth the Lives – great gods and spiritual forces, *Cosmocratores*, who become the intelligent architects and builders of the manifold parts of the universe. From their own individual spiritual essence, other lesser hierarchies are begotten, and these in turn emanate or evolve from themselves still other groups. These are they which represent in the hidden depths of the psyche those primordial ideas which Jung speaks of as archetypal images ever present in the collective unconscious of the race.

Thus it is that through the union of the human consciousness with the being of the gods in an ascending scale the soul of man may gradually approach the final root and source of his being. In the Buddhist scheme this is 'the essence of mind which is intrinsically pure', the *Dharmakaya*, the unconditioned divine body of truth. The intent to frighten malignant demons has no inclusion within the scope of this technique. Whether the latter hypothesis is original with Major Waddell or not is difficult to surmise, though the thesis is common to all primitive peoples. Probably it was made by a Lama in a lighter vein to put an end to leading questions; though at the same time it is true that in moments of psychic danger, the assumption of a god-form is of enormous assistance. Not because the threatening elemental or demon, for example, is fooled or frightened by the form. But because the operator, in opening himself to one phase of the divine spirit by the assumption of its symbolic form, does take upon himself or is empowered with the authority and dominion of that god.

It was in Egypt, so far as the western form of magic is concerned, that these cosmic forces received close attention and their qualities and attributes observed and recorded. Thus arose the conventionalized pictographs of their gods which are profound in significance, while simple in the moving eloquence of their description It is the Egyptian god-forms that are used in occidental magic, not those of Tibet or India. The technical use of these god-forms consists in the application of the powers of will and imagination – as well as of sound and colour. A very profound paragraph may be found in *The Mahatma Letters*, where K.H. wrote to A.P. Sinnett: 'How could you make yourself understood – command in fact those semi-intelligent forces, whose means of communicating with us are not through spoken words but through sounds and colours, in correlations between the vibrations of the two. For sound, light and colour are the main factors in forming these grades of intelligence ...'

Though it is hardly politic to enter more deeply into this matter, the remarks of K.H. apply equally to other forces and powers than elemental. The astral form of colour and light assumed in the imagination creates a mould or a focus of a special kind into which, by technical modes of vibration and invocation, the force or spiritual power desired incarnates. By the clothing of one's own astral form with the ideal figure of the god, now vitalized by the descent of the invoked force, it is held that man may be assumed or exalted into the very bosom of godhead, and so gradually return, with the acquisition of his own humanity, to that unnameable mysterious Root wherefrom originally he came.

Sound in Magical Conjurations

Another instance of Waddell's lack of humour and insight occurs on page 322. In describing the training of the novice, it is said that the Lama adopts a 'deep hoarse voice, acquired by training in order to convey the idea that it emanates from maturity and wisdom.' It is not known to me whether any of my readers have witnessed any kind of a magical ceremony, or heard an invocation recited by a skilled practitioner – though I should say few have. The tone always adopted is one which will yield the maximum of vibration. For many students a deep intoning, or a humming, is the one which vibrates the most. Therefore that is the ideal tone whereby to awaken from within the subtle magical forces required. It will have been noted too that the best invocations are always sonorous and intensely vibrant. The idea that the voice should suggest maturity and wisdom is merely silly. This is another instance of western contempt rather than a sympathetic attempt really to understand a foreign system. The Tibetan specimens of ritual given by Waddell contain an amusing number of *Oms, Hums, Has*, and *Phats*, but then western conjurations contain equally amusing barbarous names of evocation – *Yah, Agla*, etc.

With this question of sound in magical conjurations I have dealt at some length elsewhere. Suffice to remark here that in *The Secret Doctrine* Madame Blavatsky suggests that the vibratory use of conjurations and sound generally have a profound significance. 'Sound and rhythm', she observes, 'are closely related to the four elements ... Such or another vibration in the air is sure to awaken corresponding powers, union with which produces good or bad results, as the case may be.' The whole subject of sound, and the employment of so-called barbarous names of evocation, requires thoroughly to be studied before one dare suggest an explanation accusing either Magi or Lamas merely of a *pose* of wisdom.

The Qabalistic Cross

One notes with aroused attention too that the Tibetans have a form of what is called here in the occident the Qabalistic Cross. On page 423 of his book, there is the following description:

Before commencing any devotional exercise, the higher Lamas perform or go through a manoeuvre bearing a close resemblance to 'crossing oneself' as practised by Christians. The Lama gently touches his forehead either with the finger or with the bell, uttering the mystic Om, then he touches the top of his chest, uttering Ah, then the epigastrium (pit of stomach) uttering Hum. And some Lamas add Sva-ha, while others complete the cross by touching the left shoulder, uttering Dam and then Yam. It is alleged that the object of these manipulations is to concentrate the parts of the Sattva, namely the body, speech, and mind upon the image or divinity which he is about to commune with.

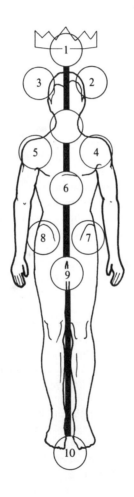

Physical Attributions of the Ten *Sephiroth*.

Prior to commenting upon the above, it is imperative to indicate certain fundamental theories to be found in some books of the Qabalah. If the reader is familiar with Dr Wm. W. Westcott's splendid *Introduction to the Study of the Kaballah* or with Dion Fortune's book *The Mystical Qabalah* he will have seen there a diagram attributing the ten *Sephiroth* to the figure of a man. Above the head, forming a crown, is *Keser* which represents the divine spirit, and at the feet is *Malkus*, while to the right and left shoulders are attributed *Gevurah* and *Gedulah*, Mars and Jupiter, Power and Majesty. In Qabalistic pneumatology, *Keser* is a correspondence of the Monad, the dynamic and essential selfhood of a man, the spirit which seeks experience through incarnation here on earth.

That this *Sephirah* or potency is placed *above* the head rather than, say, within the brain or in the centre of the heart, is highly significant. It is the light of the spirit which shines always into the darkness below. ('The spirit of man is the candle of the Lord.' And again, 'When his candle shined upon my head and by his light I walked through darkness.') This is an idea which has its parallels in other systems too. For example, in *The Epitome of Theosophy* we find Judge writing: 'It is held that the real man, who is the higher self, being the spark of the Divine, overshadows the visible being, which has the possibility of becoming united to that spark. Thus it is said that the higher Spirit is not in the man, but above him.'

All mystical and magical procedure has as its object so to purify the lower self that this higher self which normally only overshadows us and is seldom in full incarnation, may descend into a purified and consecrated vehicle. The theurgic tradition asserts that, by the proper performance of the Qabalistic Cross, amongst other things, this end may be accomplished. As a devotional exercise or meditation, it is used in collaboration with the formulation of certain lineal figures, the vibration of names of power, and followed by the invocation of the four great archangels. Its western form is as follows:

1. Touch the forehead, and say *Atoh* (Thou art)
2. Touch the breast, say *Malkus* (the Kingdom)
3. Touch the right shoulder, say *ve-Gevurah* (and the Power)
4. Touch the left shoulder, say *ve-Gedulah* (and the Glory)
5. Clasping the hands over the heart, say *le-Olahm, Amen* (for ever, Amen.)
6. Here follow suitable Pentagrams made facing the cardinal quarters, and the vibration of names of power.
7. Extend the arms in the form of a cross, saying:
8. Before me Raphael, behind me Gabriel.
9. On my right hand Michael, on my left hand Auriel.
10. For before me flames the Pentagram.

11. And behind me shines the six-rayed Star.

12. Repeat 1-5, the Qabalistic Cross.

So far as this little ritual is concerned, one may describe its action as under several heads. It first invokes the power of the higher self as a constant source of surveillance and guidance. It places the subsequent procedures under the divine aegis. Having then banished by the tracing of the appropriate pentagrams all non-essential beings from the four cardinal points with the aid of the four four-lettered names of God, it then calls the four Archangels – the four concretized functions of the interior psychic world, and the dual pair of opposites – to protect the sphere of magical operation that is the circle of the self. In closing, it once again invokes the higher self, so that from the beginning to the end, the entire ceremony is under the guardianship of the spirit. The first section, comprising points one to five, identifies the higher self of the operator with the highest aspects of the Sephirotic universe. In fact, it affirms the soul's essential identity with the collective consciousness of the whole of mankind.

If one attempted a further analysis, the Hebrew Word *Atoh*, meaning 'Thou', would refer to the divine white brilliance, the higher self overshadowing each man. By drawing down the Light to the pit of the stomach – which symbolically represents the feet, since to bend down to the feet would make an awkward gesture – the vertical shaft of a cross of light is established in the imagination. The horizontal shaft is affirmed by touching both the shoulders, and vibrating words which state that the qualities of the higher self include both power and majesty, severity and loving-kindness. Equilibrium is the especial characteristic of the cross as a particular symbol, and the tracing of the Qabalistic Cross within the aura affirms the descent of the spirit and its equilibrium within consciousness or within the magical sphere. This meaning is further emphasized by the gesture of clasping the hands over the *Tipharas* centre, the heart place of harmony and balance, and saying *le-Olahm, Amen,* forever.

The Sanskrit word *Sattva* implies purity and rhythm and harmony, and of the three *Gunas* or qualities refers to spirit. Similarly in the western equivalent of this schema, alchemy, the three qualities are correspondences of the three major alchemical principles, salt, sulphur and mercury. Of these the Universal Mercury is an attribution of *Keser* – that holy angel who is the divine guardian and Watcher, overshadowing the soul of man, ever awaiting an ordered approach so that its vehicle may be lifted up to its own glory. There is here, then, a very great resemblance between the Tibetan devotional exercise and that which is enjoined as one of the most important practices of the Qabalistic Magic of the occidental tradition.

Lamaism and the Eucharist

In that section of the book where Waddell describes the Lamaistic celebration of the Eucharist, another important parallelism is to be found. It describes how the priest or lama who conducts the ceremony is obliged to have purified himself during the greater part of the preceding twenty-four hours by ceremonial bathing, and by having uplifted his mind through continual repetition of mantras or invocations. The actual description of the inner or magical aspect of the ritual, while not particularly well stated, is given for what it is worth: 'Everything being ready and the congregation assembled, the priest, ceremonially pure by the ascetic rites above noted, and dressed in robe and mantle, abstracts from the great image of the Buddha *Amitayus* part of the divine essence of that deity, by placing the *vajra* of his *rdor jehti t'ag* upon the nectar vase which the image of *Amitayus* holds in his lamp, and applying the other end to his own bosom, over his heart. Thus, through the string, as by a telegraph wire passes the divine spirit, and the Lama must mentally conceive that his heart is in actual union with that of the god *Amitayus* and that, for the time being, he is himself that god.'

After this meditation, the rice-offering and the fluid in a special vase are consecrated by very 'fierce' invocations and cymbal music. Then the consecrated food and water is partaken of by the assembly.

From the theurgic viewpoint the rationale of the Eucharist is quite simple. There may be innumerable types of Eucharist, all having different ends in view. A substance is chosen having a special affinity according to the doctrine of sympathies for a particular kind of spiritual force or god and ceremonially consecrated. Thus a wheaten wafer is of the substance of the corn goddess, attributed either to the powers of Venus, or the element of earth, presided over by Ceres or Persephone. Penetrative oils would be specially referred to the element of fire, the tutelary deity of which is Horus. Olives would be sacred to the force represented by the astrological sign Aquarius, the element air, and the goddess Hathor. And wine is referred to Dionysius and the solar gods generally, Osiris, Ra, etc.

By an elaborate table of correspondences it is possible to select any substance to be the physical basis for the manifestation of a spiritual idea. The consecration, ceremonially, of the material basis by means of an invocation of the divine force accomplishes what is vulgarly called the miracle of transubstantiation. To use more preferable magical terminology, the substance is transformed from a dead inert body into a living organism, a talisman in short. The consecration charges it and gives it a soul, as it were.

Talismanic Magic

At this juncture, I must register my emphatic disagreement with those writers on science and Magic who, impressed unduly or in the wrong way by modern psychology, explain the effect of a talisman as due entirely to suggestion. This is sheer nonsense. And I can only assume that whoever makes this sort of argument is without the least experience of this type of magical work. It is this kind of experience which comprises or should comprise the first part of one's early practical work in the technical side of Magic. And lack of experience in even this elementary aspect of technical virtuosity vitiates every opinion on other forms.

We are confronted here by the same problem that arose over a century ago in another sphere. The early great magnetisers after Mesmer − great names like de Puysegur, Deleuze, du Potet and Lafontaine − claimed that by means of will and imagination they were able to open themselves to an influx from without and then to transmit from their own organisms a species of vital power or animal magnetism. This force pervading all space they claimed could be used therapeutically. Later on, when attempting to appropriate the trance phenomena and healing methods inaugurated by the mesmerists, physicians of the orthodox school eliminated the theory of an actual transmissible force and in its stead employed the theory of suggestion. Beginning with Braid and continuing through a line of very fine investigators, a duplication of magnetic phenomena was achieved purely by psychological means without recourse to any hypothesis of animal magnetism.

But because phenomena can be produced by one method does not necessarily imply that its duplication by another is false. It may well be that similar feats can be accomplished by quite separate techniques based upon differing hypotheses − each valid in its own sphere and each capable of explaining one set of facts. In any event, the reality of animal magnetism, or the transmission of what in the East has been termed *prana*, vitality, has never been disproved.

On the contrary, it is a simple matter to prove it quite adequately. Let any normal healthy person suspend his fingers over the arm of a second person, imagining and willing that his *prana* courses out from his fingers in long filmy streamers of energy. If the second person sits quite still and cultivates an objectivity of feeling and waiting, he will soon sense either a cold draught on that arm or a tingling in his own finger tips which proceeds from the influx of *prana*. This is an experience quite apart from suggestion, for it may be attempted with those who have no idea of the fundamental principles involved and who, therefore, are not directly susceptible to suggestion on this score. Spontaneously, and without prompting, they will observe the fact that a tangible transmission of vitality has been effected. It should be possible to test it by some very delicate instrument. Moreover, in a dark room, these streamers issuing from the fingers can be readily seen if the hand is held in front of a black cloth.

Furthermore, one's ability to generate this power is capable of culture. I have elaborated this theme from the point of view of auto-therapy in *The Art of True Healing* (see page 137). And it is also my suggestion that the interested reader consult Dr Bernard Hollander's work *Hypnotism* and *Self-Hypnotism* where the problems of suggestion and animal magnetism are discussed at some length in connection with experimental work – and that most intelligently.

Briefly, let me say that suggestion does not invalidate in the least the fact of animal magnetism, nor the effect of a charged talisman. For, as I have intimated, we are confronted by the same problem that years earlier had arisen as to whether the trance and therapeutic phenomena of mesmerism were indeed due to suggestion or to a surcharge of vitality. If power can be passed to an individual as I contend it can, why not to some specific substance which is particularly appropriate in its nature to receiving a charge? Tradition has always asserted that metals, gems and precious stones, vellum and parchment make good material bases for talismans. If the vitality of the operator be augmented by simple meditation exercises such as have been described in *The Art of True Healing*, or by the straightforward magical methods of invocation and visualization of god-forms, then a very powerful charge is imparted to the material basis of the talisman.

Of itself, however, the talisman is nothing. It only becomes efficacious when properly consecrated and vitalized. Thus the Eucharistic substance is worthless as such until it has been duly consecrated by an appropriate magical ceremony, and transformed into the vehicle of an appropriate type of force.

Consecration

The mode of consecration is, of course, another matter, not to be described here inasmuch as it is a lengthy and technical business. One of the important parts of such a ceremony for the consecration of a talisman or a Eucharistic substance, is the assumption of the god-form astrally. When the operator has determined the nature of the divine force he is desirous to invoke, and having selected the material substance congruous in nature to that force, he must endeavour during his ceremony of consecration so to exalt the spirit within him that he actually becomes identified, in one way or another, with the consciousness of that particular force or deity. The more thorough and complete is this dynamic union, the more automatic and simple does the mere subsequent charging of the telesmata become. In the case of the Eucharist the idea, however, is not only spiritual identification with the deity as a preliminary to the ascent to the unknown universal God, but the alchemical transmutation of the lower vehicles into a glorified body.

While the higher consciousness of the Magus may certainly be dissolved in ecstasy, it becomes imperative to create a magical link between that divine consciousness and his physical body and emotions. Therefore, the ceremonial magnetizing of a material substance, be it a wafer or wine or herb, impregnates it with that same divine force. Its consumption assumes that transmuting force into the very being and fibre of the Magus, to carry out the work of transformation. As the pseudonymous Therion once wrote: 'The magician becomes filled with God, fed upon God, intoxicated with God. Little by little his body will become purified by the internal lustration of God; day by day his mortal frame, shedding its earthly elements, will become in very truth the Temple of the Holy Ghost. Day by day matter is replaced by Spirit, the human by the divine; ultimately the change will be complete; God manifest in flesh will be his name.'

It requires some little magical experience fully to appreciate this, but this simplified explanation will I think throw more light on the actual nature of the ceremony than does the description of Waddell.

I do not wish to discuss in more than a few words the validity of a Eucharistic ceremony celebrated other than by the operator himself. Bearing in mind that a properly performed Eucharistic ceremony results in the production of a talisman, it becomes clear that this kind of operation is principally of benefit to him who performs it. It seems to my way of thinking a useless rite to partake of the Eucharist *en bloc*. The Buddha is supposed to have remarked that no ceremonies are of the least avail in obtaining salvation or redemption. To me, it seems not that he attacked the magical tradition in these words, but rather wholesale ceremonies in which the audience plays no active part at all. There is no willed stimulation of their own spiritual principles – it is a passive vicarious participation in the labours of other people. Magic, with Buddhism, agrees with Madame Blavatsky's dictum that 'the pivotal doctrine of the Esoteric philosophy admits no privileges or speical gifts in man save those won by his own ego through personal effort and merit ...'

The Tibetan Mystery Plays

There is one final topic I should like to refer to at some length before leaving this comparative study. In so doing it is necessary to leave Waddell for the moment to refer to the writings of two other Tibetan scholars, Madame Alexandra David Neel and Dr W.Y. Evans Wentz. Both of these scholars have written with sympathy and understanding on Tibetan religion and magical practices. The subject to be considered is a Tibetan mystery play in relation to Western magical ritual.

Chöd is a kind of mystery drama, and the magician or yogi is the sole actor therein. Dr Evans Wentz, in his masterly introduction to the translation of the play or ritual in *Tibetan Yoga and Secret Doctrines*, explains that,

> The *Chöd* rite is, first of all, a mystic drama, performed by a single human actor, assisted by numerous spiritual beings, visualized, or imagined, as being present in response to his magic invocation. Its stage setting is in some wild awe-inspiring locality, often in the midst of the snowy fastnesses of the Tibetan Himalayas, twelve to fifteen or more thousand feet above sea-level. Commonly by preference it is in a place where corpses are chopped to bits and given to the wolves and vultures. In the lower altitudes of Bhutan and Sikkim, a densely wooded jungle solitude may be chosen; but in countries wherein corpses are cremated, such as Nepal and India, a cremation-ground is favoured. Cemeteries or localities believed to be haunted by malignant and demoniacal spirits are always suitable.
>
> Long probationary periods of careful preparation under a master of *Chöd* are required before the novice is deemed fit or is allowed to perform the psychically dangerous rite ... At the outset, the celebrant of the *Chöd* Rite is directed to visualize himself as being the Goddess of the All-Fulfilling (or All-Performing Wisdom) by whose occult will he is mystically empowered; and then, as he sounds the thigh-bone trumpet, invoking the *gurus* and the different orders of spiritual beings, he begins the ritual dance, with mind and energy entirely devoted to the one supreme end of realizing, as the Mahayana teaches, that *Nirvana* and the *Sangsara* are, in reality, an inseparable unity.
>
> Stanzas three to seven inclusive suggest the profound symbolism underlying the ritual; and this symbolism, as will be seen, is dependent upon the Five Directions, the corresponding Five 'Continents' of the *lamaic* cosmography with their geometrical shapes, the Five Passions (hatred, pride, lust, jealousy, stupidity) which the *yogin* triumphantly treads under foot in the form of demons, and the Five Wisdoms, the antidotes to the Five Passions ... In the ninth stanza comes the dramatic spearing of the elements of Self with the spears of the Five Orders of *Dakinis*.

As the Mystery proceeds, and the *yogin* prepares for the mystic sacrifice of his own fleshly form, there is revealed the real significance of the *Chöd* or 'cutting off'.

Thus the *Chöd* as explained by Evans Wentz is seen as a highly intricate magical ceremony in which the lama, identifying himself with a goddess through the visualized assumption of her astral or ideal form, invokes what we in the west would call angels, spirits and elementals to attend upon his ceremony. These he deliberately invites to enter his own sphere. No longer does he act, as in other specialized forms of invocation, by selecting one particular force only and attempting forcibly to keep all others out from his sphere of consciousness. Now he makes a vacuum as it were; he opens himself completely, and wholly receptive permits whatever influences will to permeate him through and through, and partake of his nature.

In one sense, he sacrifices his being to them. His mind, his emotions and feelings, and the organs and limbs of his physical body, and the minute cells and lives composing them, are all handed over to the invaders for consumption, if so they wish. 'For ages, in the course of renewed births I have borrowed from countless living beings – at the cost of their welfare and life – food, clothing, all kinds of services to sustain my body, to keep it joyful in comfort and to defend it against death. Today, I pay my debt, offering for destruction this body which I have held so dear. I give my flesh to the hungry, my blood to the thirsty, my skin to clothe those who are naked, my bones as fuel to those who suffer from cold. I give happiness to the unhappy ones. I give my breath to bring back the dying to life.'

It is, briefly, a very idealized form of personal sacrifice in which the whole individuality is opened up, hypothetically, to whatever desires to possess it. As a magical operation it must rank very high in technical virtuosity, and for him who is sufficiently endowed with the magical gifts to perform it a most effectual ritual so far as results are concerned.

The final stage of the drama is ably described by Mme. David Neel in this passge:

Now he must imagine that he has become a heap of charred human bones that emerges from a lake of black mud – the mud of misery, of moral defilement, and of harmful deeds to which he has co-operated during the course of numberless lives, whose origin is lost in the night of time. He must realize that the very idea of sacrifice is but an illusion, an offshoot of blind, groundless pride. In fact, he *has nothing* to give away, because he *is nothing*. These useless bones, symbolizing the destruction of his phantom. 'I', may sink into the muddy lake, it will not matter. That silent renunciation of the ascetic who realizes that he holds nothing that he can renounce, and who utterly relinquishes the elation springing from the idea of sacrifice, closes the rite.

The Role of the Ego

In attempting a comparison between this *Chöd* rite and European magical rituals, we are at the outset confronted not by the problem of inferiority of conception or technical skill, as many have heretofore thought, but by a vast difference of metaphysical outlook. That is to say, there is a markedly enunciated opposition both of philosophic and pragmatic aim. In common with all schools and sects of Buddhism, the Mahayana is directly antagonistic to the ego idea. The whole of its philosophy and ethical code is directly concerned with the elimination of the 'I' thinking. It holds that this is purely a fantasy bred of childish ignorance, very much as the mediaeval notion that the sun circumambulated the earth was the result of imperfect knowledge. Therefore the whole of its religious and philosophic scheme is directed towards uprooting this fantasy from the thinking of its disciples. This is the *Anatta* doctrine, and its importance to Buddhism is grounded in the belief that from this fantasy spring all sorrow and unhappiness.

European Magic, on the other hand, owes its fundamental doctrines to the Qabalah. Whilst having much in common with the broad outlines of Buddhism, the metaphysics of the Qabalah are essentially egocentric in a typically European way. Nevertheless, the terms of its philosophy are so general that they may be interpreted freely from a variety of angles. Whilst decrying the ills and limitations that accompany the false ego sense, it emphasizes not so much the destruction of the ego as, with true western practicality, its purification and integration. It is a very useful instrument when it has been taught the needful lesson that it is not identical with the self, but only one particular instrument, one small phase of activity comprised within the large sphere of the total individual. Hence, the practical theurgy that arises as a superstructure from the basic theoretical Qabalah must also be affected by such a viewpoint. Instead of seeking to remove the ego as such, it seeks to extend the limited borders of its horizon, to enlarge its scope of activity, to improve its vision and its spiritual capacity. In a word, so to enhance its psychological worth that in taking cognisance of the universal Self permeating all things, it may become identified with that Self. Here, then, is a fundamental distinction in the point of view envisaged.

The Bornless Ritual

Just as the *Chöd* has its roots in the primitive *Bön* animism of pre-Buddhistic Tibet, having been very clearly re-shaped by the Mahayanists, so the western ritual I propose to consider here also has a very crude origin. It dates possibly to the centuries immediately preceding our own Christian era. 'The Bornless Ritual', which is the name it has come to be known by, may be found in its elementary form in *Fragments of a Graeco-Egyptian Work upon Magic*, published in 1852 for the Cambridge Antiquarian Society by Charles Wycliffe Goodwin, M.A. The ritual has since undergone considerable transformation. From a simple primitive prayer to ward off evil, in the hands of skillful theurgists trained in the western tradition of the Golden Dawn, it has been evolved into a highly complex but most effectual and inspiring work. The ritual, as such, now consists of a lengthy proem, five elemental invocations, and an eloquent peroration. Sandwiched between them is a Eucharistic ceremony.

In the prologue, the operator identifies himself with Osiris by means of the visualized assumption of the Egyptian god-form. That is to say, he formulates about him the form of Osiris. His imagination must be pictorially keen and vivid enough to visualize even the smallest details of dress and ornamentation in clear and bright colour and form. As a result of this effort, if he is successful, no longer is the ceremony conducted by a mere human being. On the contrary, the invocations and commands issue forth from the very mouth of godhead.

Osiris in magical symbolism is human consciousness itself, when finally it has been purified, exalted, and integrated – the human ego as it stands in a balanced position between heaven and earth, reconciling and uniting both. In a Golden Dawn initiation ritual, one officer, whilst assuming the astral mask of the god, defines its nature by affirming: 'I am Osiris, the Soul in twin aspect, united to the higher by purification, perfected by suffering, glorified through trial. I have come where the great Gods are, through the Power of the Mighty Name.'

The lama, when performing the *Chöd* rite, likewise imagines himself to be one of the *dakinis*, The Goddess of the All-Fulfilling Wisdom. She, so runs the interpretation of Madame Alexandra David Neel, represents esoterically the higher will of the lama. The concepts of both rituals actually are very similar.

But here the resemblance, superficial indeed, ends. For in the *Chöd* ritual the lama or hermit, invoking the various orders of demons and spirits, identifies them with his own vices and so sacrifices himself. He sees his ego comprised of hatred or wrath, pride, lust, jealousy and stupidity, and throws these qualities to the invading spirits and demons for consumption. He visualizes his body as a corpse being dismembered by the wrathful goddess, and its organs also being preyed upon by a host of malignant entities. In a few words, a species of dissociation is intentionally induced.

Now in the western system, the various orders of elementals are also invoked from their stations during this Bornless Ritual. But they are commanded to flow through the Magus with a view, not to preying upon him and thus destroying him, but to purify him. The intent is totally different. At each station or cardinal quarter, the appropriate tutelary deity is invoked by means of the formulation of the astral form and the proper lineal figures. In the East, as a result of the vibration of the appropriate barbarous names of evocation that 'have a power ineffable in the sacred rites', and by enunciating the Words of Power, the Sylphs rush through his sphere of sensation like a gentle zephyr blowing the foul dust of pride before them. The Salamanders, raging from the South, consume with a burning fire the jealousy and hatred within him. Lust and passion become purified by the Undines invoked from the West, as though the Magus were immersed in purest water from which he issues spotless and consecrated. Whilst the Gnomes, coming from the North, cleanse him from sloth and stupidity, exactly as muddy and impure water is cleansed by being filtered through sand. The operator, all the while, is conscious of the injunction *a propos* the elementals given in one of his initiations. Or rather, the injunction has become a part of his unconscious outlook upon life. 'Be thou, therefore, prompt and active as the Sylphs, but avoid frivolity and caprice. Be energetic and strong as the Salamanders but avoid irritability and ferocity. Be flexible and attentive to images like the Undines, but avoid idleness and changeability. Be laborious and patient like the Gnomes, but avoid grossness and avarice. So shalt thou gradually develop the powers of thy soul, and fit thyself to command the spirits of the elements.'

The elemental invocations over – very difficult work, to do which requires at least seventy or eighty minutes of intense magical concentration – the operator, being convinced of the presence of the invoked force and the salutary effect of their respective purifications upon him, begins the second stage of his work by invoking the fifth element, the alchemical quintessence, *Akasa* or the Ether, in both its negative and positive aspects. The effect of these two invocations is to equilibriate the elementals already commanded to the scene of operations. Also, it tends to provide an etheric mould or astral vacuum into which the higher spiritual forces may descend to make contact with the unconscious psyche of the operator.

At this juncture it is customary to celebrate the mystic repast which again seems the reverse in intention of the *Chöd* banquet. At least, the reversal is only apparent. The Magus celebrates the Eucharist of the four elements, after reciting powerfully the Enochian invocation of the mystical tablet of Union beginning *Ol Sonuf vaorsagi goho Iada balta* – 'I reign over you, saith the God of Justice ...' The perfume of the rose on the altar, the low fire of the lighted lamp, the bread and salt, and the wine are thus powerfully charged with the divine force. So that as he partakes of the elements, the influx of the spirit elevates not only his own ego but all the innumerable cells and lives which comprise his own lower vehicles of manifestation. And more too, for it affects all the spiritual beings, angels, elementals, and spirits who, in answer to invocation, now pervade his astral sphere. Thus he accomplishes that which the tenets of all mystical religions enjoin, the elevation of all the inferior lives as man himself evolves. This he does, in this case, by the agency of the magical invocations and the Eucharist, so that not only does he himself become blessed by the impact of the divine spirit, but so do all the other beings present partake with him of the glory. There is no witholding of blessing. For here, as in the *Chöd* rite, there is no retention of power from any being.

At the opening of the ceremony, all forces and all beings whatsoever are carefully banished by the appropriate banishing rituals so as to leave a clean and holy space for the celebration of the ceremony. But into this consecrated sphere all the orders of elementals, comprised within the five-fold division of things, are called. And it is this mighty host who, having purified the sphere of the magus by having consumed the undesirable elements within him, are consecrated and blessed by the Eucharist and the descent of the refulgent Light. The whole operation is sealed by the peroration:

I am He! The Bornless Spirit, having sight in the feet! Strong and the Immortal Fire! I am He the Truth! I am He who hate that evil should be wrought in the world! I am He that lighteneth and thundereth! I am He whose mouth ever flameth! I am He, the Begetter and Manifester unto the Light! I am He, the Grace of the World! 'The Heart girt with a Serpent' is my Name.

It coincides with the re-formulation of the god-form of Osiris. And with each clause of the final hymn, the magician makes the effort in imagination to realize that they answer to the divine qualities and characteristics of the god, whose light is even now descending upon him. The end result is illumination and ecstasy, a transporting of the consciousness of the magus to an identity with the consciousness of all that lives, an ineffable union with the Light, the One Life that permeates all space and time.

It will be conceded I hope that the western conceptions of Magic are in no way inferior, as so many unfortunately have come in the past several years to believe, to those prevalent in Tibet and the East. It is only that the philosophic forms are somewhat different. And this difference has its root in varying psychological needs – and these at no time are irreconcilable.

Theurgy and Spiritual Development

Here then I must content myself with these comparisons between various points of magical interest common to both East and West. My desire to compare them sprang originally from a persual of Major Waddell's really erudite book – where the reader may find other items of great and absorbing interest. But I do feel that unless he has the magical key to these practices and various ceremonies which the Lamas perform, he is apt to be bored and left without a proper understanding of them. With all due respect to the eastern wisdom for which assuredly I have a great and profound reverence, it is my belief that in this instance a study of Theurgy as developed by western genius is more capable than aught else of throwing an illuminating ray on the true nature of spiritual development by means of the path of Magic. There are many paths to the one goal of the Beatific Vision. Of these paths, meditation is one. Probably in its development of meditation and the purely introspective processes of Yoga, the East is far in advance of the West. Certainly there is no better text-book on that subject than the Patanjali Yoga Aphorisms. And I appreciate the fact that Blavatsky brought Theosophy from the East. But Theurgy has climbed to sun-illuminated heights in the western schools. Our hidden sanctuaries of initiation, where Magic has long been successfully employed, but all too rigidly suppressed from the notice of the outer world, have a finer, nobler and more spiritual interpretation than any to be found in Eastern systems.

For myself, I can only say that experience demonstrates that Theurgy makes no confusion in its statement of ideals. It introduces no superstitious chaos concerning the fear of demons, etc., which is only too apparent in the Tibetan scheme, judging from Waddell's book. Every magical effort of the Lamas is described as being due to fear or hatred of evil spirits, though I do not doubt but that many lamas have a finer understanding of their system than this. Theurgy nurtures the ideal that its technique is a means of furthering one's spiritual development so that thereby one may consummate the true objects of incarnation. Not selfishly, but that one may be the better able thereafter to help and participate in the ordered progress of mankind to that perfect day when the glory of this world passes, and the Sun of Wisdom shall have arisen to shine over the splendid sea.

2. The Art of Magic

Of all the subects that comprise what nowadays is called occultism, the most misunderstood of all is Magic. Even alchemy, which to some is annoyingly dark and obscure, evokes far more sympathy and understanding as a rule than does Magic. For example, the psychologist Jung has observed of alchemy in his essay *The Ego and The Unconscious* that 'it would be an unpardonable depreciation of value if we were to accept the current view, and reduce the spiritual striving of the alchemists to the level of the retort and the smelting furnace. Certainly this aspect belonged to it; it represented the tentative beginnings of exact chemistry. But it also had a spiritual side which has never yet been given its true value, and which from the psychological standpoint must not be underestimated.'

Yet Magic, strange to say, receives no such evaluation − except insofar as the term Magic is allied to the unconscious, and is said to represent a primitive attempt to cognize the unconscious. There is, hence, hardly more than the barest minimum attempt to arrive at an understanding of its processes. For the moment, I do not wish to analyse the possible reasons for this amazing phenomenon. What is more to the point, however, is to provide some more or less intelligible approach to the subject so that, given an initial glimpse of the bright light flooding the world of Magic, more people may feel disposed to devote just a little of their energies and time to its study. The advantages and benefits are such as to make this effort extremely worth while.

The Aims of Magic

Putting it simply and briefly, let me say at the outset that Magic concerns itself in the main with the world of modern psychology. That is to say, it deals with that sphere of the psyche of which normally we are not conscious but which exerts an enormous influence upon our lives. Magic is a series of psychological techniques so devised as to enable us to probe more deeply into ourselves. To what end? First, that we shall understand ourselves more completely. Apart from the fact that such self-knowledge in itself is desirable, an understanding of the inner nature releases us from unconscious compulsions and motivations and confers a mastery over life. Second, that we may the more fully express that inner self in everyday activities. It is only when mankind as a whole has reached, or perhaps when the more advanced men and women in the world have evolved, some degree of inner realization that we may ever hope for that ideal utopian condition of things – a wide tolerance, peace, and universal brotherhood. It is to ends such as these that Magic owes its *raison d'etre*.

Religion and Magic

Approaching the matter from another point of view, it may be said that Magic deals with the same problems as religion. It does not waste its or our valuable time with futile speculations with regard to the existence or nature of God. It affirms dogmatically that there is an omnipresent and eternal life principle – and thereupon, in true scientific fashion, lays down a˙host of methods for proving it for oneself. How may we know God? Here, as before, there is a well-defined and elaborate technique for dealing with the human consciousness as such and exalting it to an immediate experience of the universal spirit permeating and sustaining all things. I say advisedly that its technique is well defined. For the system has an abhorrence of the attitude of those good-natured but muddle-headed thinkers who, refusing to accept their human limitations as they are now, aim too high without dealing with the manifold problems in the way.

Let us assume that yonder building is ten storeys high. How may we reach the roof? Certainly not by ignoring the very obvious fact that at least two hundred feet intervene between us and the roof! Yet that is precisely the attitude of the so-called simplicity cult in mystical religion. God, they affirm, is an exalted state of infinite consciousness to which the microcosmic mind must be united. So far, so good – and here Magic is in accord with their view. Therefore, these people propose to attempt gaining the summit of attainment by ignoring the steps between man as we find him now and the supreme end – God. It is as though they wished to jump from the ground to the roof of the aforesaid building.

Magic adopts a slightly different attitude. It is one, however, which is markedly similar to the commonsense attitude of the mythical man in the street. To get to the top of the building we must either climb the various flights of stairs leading there, or else take the lift upwards. In either case, it is a graduated process – an evolution, if you wish.

Man, holds the magical theory, is a more or less complicated creature whose several faculties of feeling, sensation, and thinking have slowly been evolved in the course of aeons of evolution. It is fatal to ignore these faculties, for evidently they were evolved for some useful purpose in answer to some inner need. Hence, in aspiring towards divine union, surely a laudable goal, we must be quite sure that our method, whatever it is, takes into consideration those faculties and develops them to the stage where they too may participate in the experience. If evolution is held up as a suitable process, then the whole man must evolve, and not simply little bits or aspects of him, whilst other parts of his nature are left undeveloped at a primitive or infantile level of being. Moreover, these faculties must be so trained as to be able to 'take' the enormous tension sure to be imposed upon them by so exalted but nevertheless so powerful an attainment. Each faculty must be deliberately trained and carried stage by stage through various levels of human and cosmic consciousness so that gradually they become accustomed to the high potential of energy, ideation, and inspiration that must inevitably accompany illumination and an extension of consciousness. Failure to consider such a viewpoint in terms of its dynamics undoubtedly must account for the catastrophes so frequently encountered in occult and mystical circles.

To present a bird's-eye view of the entire field of Magic, let me summarily state that for convenience the subject may be divided into at least three major divisions. One – Divination. Two – Evocation and Vision. Three – Invocation. I will define each separately and at some little length.

Divination

With regard to the first division, the magical hypothesis is quite definite. It holds that divination is not ultimately concerned with mere fortune-telling – nor even with divining the spiritual causes in the background of material events, though this latter is of no little importance. On the contrary, however, the practice of divination when conducted aright has as its objective the development of the inner psychic faculty of intuition. It is an enormous asset spiritually to have developed an exquisite sensitivity to the inner subtle world of the psyche. When carried on for a sufficiently long period of time, the practice builds slowly but efficiently a species of bridge between the consciousness of man and that deeper hidden part of his psyche of which usually he is not aware – the unconscious, or higher self. In these deeper spiritual aspects of his nature are the divine roots of discrimination, spiritual discernment, and lofty wisdom.

The object of divination is quite simply, then, the construction of a psychic mechanism whereby this source of inspiration and life may be made accessible to the ordinary consciousness, to the ego. That this mechanism is concerned at the outset with providing answers to apparently trivial questions is by itself no objection to the technique itself. The preliminary approaches to any study may seem unworthy of or incompatible with that study. And divination is no exception to

the general trend. Nor is the objection valid that the technique is open
to frequent abuse by unscrupulous charlatans. But practised sincerely
and intelligently and assiduously by the real student, consciousness
gradually opens itself to a deeper level of awareness. 'The brain
becomes porous to the recollections and dictates of the soul', (to use a
current theosophical expression) is a true statement of the actual
results of the training. As the object of analytical psychology is the
assimilation of the repressed content of the unconscious to the
ordinary wake-a-day consciousness, so by these other magical means
the human mind becomes aware of itself as infinitely vaster, deeper
and wiser than ever it realized before. A sense of the spiritual aspect of
things dawns upon the mind — a sense of one's own innate high
wisdom, and a recognition of divinity working through man and the
universe. Surely such a viewpoint elevates divination above the level of
a mere occult art to an intrinsic part of mystical endeavour?

Geomancy, Tarot and Astrology

These are the fundamental techniques of the divinatory system.
Geomancy is divination by means of earth. At one time, its
practitioners actually used sand or black earth in which to trace its
sigils and symbols – a typically primitive or mediaeval method. Today
geomantic diviners use pencil and paper, relying upon graphite in their
pencils to formulate, theoretically, a magical link between themselves
and the so-called divining intelligences or elementals of earth. It is, so
far as my own experience goes, a highly efficient technique, and I can
claim at least an 80 per cent degree of accuracy over several years.

Tarot is the name of a set of cards, seventy-eight in number, which
were introduced into Europe in either the fourteenth or fifteenth
century. No one knows where they came from. Their origin is a
complete mystery. At one period in Europe there were no such cards
available, so far as we can see. At another time, the cards were
circulating freely.

Little mention need be made of astrology, since that has long been
one of the most popular methods with which the public has been made
familiar. Anyone who practises these methods with this objective in
mind will assuredly become aware of the results I have described. And
while, it is true, his querents for divination may receive perfectly good
answers to the questions they have asked, departing from his
threshold in the spirit of gratitude and wonder, the intuitive
development accruing to him will constitute the more important side
of that transaction.

Evocation

It is when we leave the relatively simple realm of divination to approach the obscure subject of evocation that we enter deep waters. Here it is that most difficulty has arisen. And it is in connection with this phase of Magic that the greatest misunderstanding and fear have developed.

In order to elucidate the matter, let me again turn to the terminology of modern psychology. The term 'complex' has achieved a fairly wide notoriety during the last quarter of a century since the circulation of the theories of Freud and Jung. It means an aggregation or group of ideas in the mind with a strong emotional charge, capable of influencing conscious thought and behaviour. If my interest is Magic, then naturally every item of information acquired, no matter what its nature, is likely to be built by association into that constellation of ideas clustering around my interest – becoming in the course of years a thoroughgoing complex. Mrs Jones my dairywoman, because of her professional predilection, will have her complex centring about milk and cows and butter and the price of eggs.

Over and above this definition, however, is the more subtle one of a group of ideas or feelings congregating about a significant or dominant psychic theme, such as sex or the need to overcome inferior feelings, or some psychic wound of childhood, tying or locking up nervous energy. Thus, as a result of repression, we may find a complex of which the possessor is totally unconscious – a complex expressing itself in a sense of insecurity, obsession by morbid unreasonable fears, and persistent anxiety. Moreover, a constellation of feelings and moods and emotional reactions may exist which have become so powerful and yet so obnoxious to reason as to have become completely split off from the main stream of the personality. What modern psychology calls a complex in this sense, the ancient psychology of Magic, which had its own system of classification and nomenclature, named a Spirit. The system of classification was the Qabalistic *Sephiroth* or the ten fundamental categories of thought.

Thus, should we essay translation of terms, the sense of inferiority we might call the spirit of *Tipharas*, whose name is said to be *Soras*, inasmuch as the sun, one of its attributions or associations, is considered the planetary symbol of the individuality. Hence an affliction to the personality, which may be considered a general or rough definition of the inferiority sense, could well be referred to *Soras* – since the spirit in the case of each *Sephirah* is considered evil. That complex expressing itself in insecurity is the spirit of *Yesod* and the moon, whose name is *Chashmodai*. This sphere of *Yesod* represents the astral design or foundation imparting stability and permanence to physical shapes and forms; in a word it is a symbol of security and strength. Should we be confronted with a case where the emotions were split off from consciousness, this is the influence of the spirit of *Hod* and *Mercury*, *Taphthartharath*. Someone wallowing in emotional chaos, having refused to develop equally consciousness and the rational faculties, is subject to the spirit of *Netsach* and Venus, *Haniel*. A purely destructive or suicidal neurosis which causes one to exhibit the symptomatic tendency deliberately to break things, or to use them in attack against oneself, is of a martial quality, belonging to *Gevurah* and Mars, the spirit *Samuel*.

This, naturally, is the subjective point of view. That there is a purely objective hierarchical theory I do not deny, but that cannot be dealt with here.

How, nowadays, do we deal with the psychoneuroses in the attempt to cure them — to eliminate them from the sphere of the patient's thinking and feeling? Principally by the analytical method. We encourage the patient to narrate freely his life history, to delineate in detail his early experiences in connection with his father and mother, his reactions to brothers and sisters, to school and playmates and the entire environment. He is asked to dwell particularly on his emotional reaction to these earlier experiences, to re-live them in his imagination, to recount and analyse his feelings towards them. Moreover, his dreams at the time of analysis are subjected to a careful scrutiny. This is necessary because the dream is a spontaneous psychic activity uninterfered with by the waking consciousness. Such activity reveals present-day unconscious reactions to the stimuli of life — reactions which modify, even form his conscious outlook. In this way the patient is enabled to realize *objectively* the nature of this complex. He must detach himself from it for a short space of time. And this critical objective examination of it, this understanding of its nature and the means whereby it came into being, enables him, not once and for all, but gradually and with the passage of time, to oust it from his ways of thinking.

Magic, however, at one time proceeded according to a slightly different technique. It, too, realized how devastating were these natural but perverse ways of thinking, and how crippling was the effect they exercised on the personality. Indecision, vacillation, incapacitation of memory, anaesthesia of feeling and sense, compulsions and phobias, besides a host of physical and moral ills, are the resultants of these complexes or spirit-dominants. So completely is the patient at the mercy of obsessing moods as almost to be beside himself, thus suggesting to the vivid imagination of the ancients an actual obsession by some extraneous spirit entity. So, in order to restore man to his former efficiency, or to the standard of normality, these afflictions must be eliminated from consciousness.

Personalization of Complexes

As its first step, Magic proceeded to personalize them, to invest them with tangible shape and form, and to give them a definite name and quality. It is the nature of the psyche spontaneously to give human characteristics and nomenclature to the contents of its own mind. In doing this, the magical system receives the official blessing, if I may say so, of no less a modern psychological authority than Dr C.G. Jung. In his commentary to *The Secret of the Golden Flower*, Jung names these complexes 'autonomous partial systems'. Referring to these partial systems, he asserts: 'Being also constituents of the psychic personality, they necessarily have the character of persons. Such partial-systems appear in mental diseases where there is no psychogenic splitting of the personality (double personality), and also, quite commonly, in mediumistic phenomena.' It is, as I have said, a natural tendency of the human mind to personalize these complexes or groupings of special ideas. As another proof of this, we may cite the phenomenon of dreams, in which quite frequently the patient's psychic difficulties or complexes are given symbolically some human or animal form.

Proceeding a step further, the ancient science of Magic postulated that to eliminate this complex it was necessary to render it objective to the patient's or student's consciousness so that he might acquire some recognition of its presence. Whilst these subconscious knots of emotion, or astral spirits, are unknown and uncontrolled, the patient is unable to control them to the best advantage, to examine them thoroughly, to accept the one or to reject the other. First of all, was the hypothesis, they must acquire tangible, objective form before they may be controlled. So long as they remain intangible and amorphous and unperceived by the ego, they cannot adequately be dealt with. By a programme of formal evocation, however, the spirits of the dark underworld, or complexes of ideas inhabiting the deeper strata of unconsciousness, may be evoked from the gloom into visible appearance in the magical triangle of manifestation. Evoked in this technical way, they may be controlled by means of the transcendental symbols and formal processes of Magic, being brought within the dominion of the stimulated will and consciousness of the theurgist. In other words, they are once more assimilated into consciousness. No longer are they independent spirits roaming in the astral world, or partial systems dwelling in the unconscious, disrupting the individual's conscious life. They are brought back once more into the personality, where they become useful citizens so to speak, integral parts of the psyche, instead of outlaws and gangsters, grievous and dangerous enemies threatening psychic unity and integrity.

The Process of Evocation

How are these evoked? What is the technical process of rendering objective these autonomous partial systems? Magic parts company here with orthodox psychology. Many months of tedious analysis at enormous financial outlay are required by the present-day psychological method to deal with these problems, and few there be who are strong enough or patient enough to persist. The magical theory prefers a drastic form of emotional and mental excitation by means of a ceremonial technique. During the evocation ceremony, divine and spirit names are continuously vibrated as part of a lengthy conjuration. Circumambulations are performed from symbolic positions in the temple – these representing different strata of the unconscious, different regions of the psychic world. Breath is inhaled into the lungs, and, rather like the pranayama technique of the Hindu Yogis, manipulated by the imagination in special ways. By means of these exercises, consciousness is stimulated to such a degree as to become opened, despite itself, to the enforced upwelling of the content of the unconscious. The upwelling is not haphazard but is definitely controlled and regulated, for the Qabalists were thoroughly familiar with the ideas of suggestion and association, arranging their conjurations so that by means of association of ideas there would be suggested to the psyche the train of ideas required – and only that train.

The particular partial system is then excuded from the sphere of sensation and projected outwards. It embodies itself in so-called astral or etheric substance normally comprising the interior body which serves as the foundation or design of the physical form, and acting as the bridge between the body and the mind, of which it is the vehicle. The astral form now reflecting the partial system projected from the unconscious, attracts to itself particles of heavy incense burned copiously during the ceremony. Gradually, in the course of the ceremonial, a materialization is built up which has the shape and character of an autonomous being. It can be spoken to and it can speak. Likewise it can be directed and controlled by the operator of the ceremony. At the conclusion of the operation, it is absorbed deliberately and consciously back into the operator by the usual formula: 'And now I say unto thee, depart from hence with the blessing of [the appropriate divine name governing that particular type of complex] upon thee. And let there ever be peace between me and thee. And be thou ever ready to come and obey my will, whether it be by a ceremony or but by a gesture.'

Thus, the defect in consciousness caused by the spirit-obsession is remedied and, because of the accession to consciousness of the tremendous power and feeling involved in such a repression, the psyche of the operator is stimulated in a special way, according to the nature of the spirit.

To recapitulate: the purpose of evocation is that some portion of the human psyche which has become deficient in a more or less important quality is made intentionally to stand out, as it were. Given body and name by the power of the stimulated will and imagination and exuded astral substance, it is, to continue to use metaphor, specially nourished by the warmth and sustenance of the sun, and given water and food that it may grow and flourish.

Familiarity, of course, is requisite before this type of Magic should be attempted. It requires study and long training. Arduous and persistent toil needs to be undertaken with the appropriate formulae before one dare apply oneself to so formidable and perhaps dangerous an aspect of the magical routine. But it has this advantage over the analytical procedure. It is infinitely speedier when once the technique has been mastered and the special association tracks have been familiarized, and considerably more thorough and effective as a cathartic agent. I hope one day to see a modification of it in current use by our psychologists.

Vision

There is an important variation of this technique. At first sight, it may seem to bear but little relationship with the evocation method. But it, too, has as its objective the necessary assimilation of the unconscious content of the psyche into normal consciousness. Its object, also, is the enlarging of the horizon of the mind by enlarging the student's intellectual conceptions of the nature of the universe.

The elementary technical processes of this method call for the drawing or the painting of coloured symbols of the elements earth, air, water, fire and ether. Each of these has a different traditional symbol and colour. To earth is attributed a yellow square. Air is a blue circle. Water is a silver crescent. Fire, the red triangle, and ether is the black egg. After staring intently at the symbol of some one particular element for several seconds, and then throwing the vision to some white or neutral surface, a reflex image of the complementary colour is seen against it. This is a normal optical illusion without having in itself any special significance. The optical reflex obtained, the student is counselled to close the eyes, *imagining* that before him is the symbolic shape and complementary colour of the element being used. The shape is then to be enlarged until it seems tall enough for him to visualize himself walking through it. Then he must permit the fantasy faculty of the mind full and unimpeded play. What is particularly important is that at this stage he must vibrate certain divine and archangelic names which tradition ascribes to that particular symbol. These names may be found in the first volume of my work *The Golden Dawn*.

In this way, he enters imaginatively or clairvoyantly by means of a vision, into the elemental realm corresponding to the nature of the symbol he has chosen. By employing element after element, he acquires a sympathetic contact with the understanding of the several hierarchical planes existing within Nature, and thus widens tremendously the sphere of his consciousness.

From the psychological point of view, we might understand the magical theory to imply that the unconscious (which has been compared to the nine-tenths of an iceberg concealed under water and not at all visible) may be classified into five principal layers or sub-divisions. These five levels correspond to the five elements, the most superficial being earth, and the deepest being ether or spirit. By following such a vision or fantasy technique the candidate's ordinary consciousness is enabled to cross the otherwise impenetrable barrier subsisting between it and the unconscious. A link is formed between the two aspects of mind, a bridge is constructed, across which the psyche may pass at any moment. Entering these various psychic levels by way of an imaginative projection is analogous to forming an association track by means of which idea, inspiration, and vitality are made available to consciousness.

The vision thus obtained corresponds generally to a sort of dream, experienced, however, in a fully conscious state – one in which none of the faculties of consciousness, such as will, criticism and keen perception are in any way in abeyance. The goal of analysis, from the synthetic and constructive point of view, is accomplished readily by such means. A wide range of knowledge and feeling is thereby opened up and assimilated without strain or difficulty to the advantage and spiritual development of the individual.

Interpretation of the vision is an important factor. The neglect of interpretation may account for the intellectual sterility and spiritual emptiness so frequently observed in those who employ similar methods. Acquaintance with the methods of Jung's symbolic analysis of dreams and spontaneous fantasies may be extremely useful here, providing a useful adjunct to the Qabalistic reference of symbols to the ten *Sephiroth* of the Tree of Life. Before passing on, it is interesting to note that Jung gives towards the end of his book *Two Essays on Analytical Psychology* an account of a patient's spontaneous fantasy which is curiously similar to the tattwa technique I have just described. He calls it a '"vision" which by intense concentration was perceived on the background of consciousness, a technique that is perfected only after long practice.' It is so interesting that I am constrained to quote it here:

> I climbed the mountain and came to a place where I saw seven red stones in front of me, seven on either side, and seven behind me. I stood in the middle of this quadrangle. The stones were flat like steps. I tried to lift the four stones that were nearest to me. In doing so I discovered that these stones were the pedestals of four statues of gods which were buried upside down in the earth. I dug them up and so arranged them around me that I stood in the middle of them. Suddenly they leaned towards one another so that their heads touched, forming something like a tent over me. I myself fell to the earth, and said, 'Fall upon me if you must, for I am tired.' Then I saw that beyond, encircling the four gods, a ring of flame had formed. After a time I arose from the ground and overthrew the statues of the gods. Where they fell to the earth four trees began to grow. And now from the circle of fire blue flames shot up which began to burn the foliage of the trees. Seeing this I said, 'This must stop. I must go into the fire myself so that the leaves may not be burned.' Then I stepped into the fire. The trees disappeared and the ring of fire contracted to one immense blue flame that carried me up from the earth.

The Supreme Sacrament

Divination, evocation and vision are the preliminary techniques of Magic. We have observed that there is considerable justification of their employment – when there is adequate understanding of their meaning and technical procedure. But these are preliminary methods only. They are but steps leading to the consummation of the supreme sacrament. The inevitable end of Magic is identical to that conceived of in mysticism, union with the Godhead. Magic conceives of divinity as Spirit and Light and Love. It is an all-pervasive and omnipresent vital force, permeating all things, sustaining every life from the most minute electron to the largest nebula of mind-staggering dimensions. It is this life which is the substratum of the entirety of existence, and it is this primal consciousness in which we live and move and have our being. In the course of manifestation, cosmic centres develop within its infinitude, centres of lofty intelligence and power, whereby the cosmic

high tension may be modified and reduced to a lower key so as
ultimately to produce an objective manifestation. These cosmic
centres of life are what for the moment we may name the gods (not
spirits) — beings of enormous wisdom, power and spirituality in an
ascending hierarchical scale between us and the unknown and
unnamed God. The particular hierarchy that they form receives in
Magic a clear classification in terms of the Qabalistic Tree of Life.

In an earlier paragraph I gave the metaphor of a man striving to
reach the roof top of a several-storeyed building. Now Magic
conceives of spiritual development in an analogous way. That is to
say, it conceives a personal evolution as progressive and orderly.
Divinity is the objective we seek to reach, the roof top. We, those of us
cherishing the mystical ideal, are below on the ground. Not with one
leap may we attain the summit. An intervening distance demands to
be traversed. To reach the roof we must use either stairs or lift. By
means of the magical technique we employ the invocation of the gods,
who answer metaphorically to the stairs or lift, and attempt union with
their wider and vaster consciousness. Since they represent the several
cosmic levels of energy and mind intervening between us and the
supreme goal, as we unite ourselves in love and reverence and
surrender to them, by so much the nearer do we approach to the
ultimate source and root of all things.

Invocation

Using the plan of the Tree of Life as his guide, the magician invokes
the lower gods or archangels, as they are named in another system,
desirous of mingling his own life with, and surrendering his own being
to, the greater and more extensive life of the God. Thus, his spiritual
perceptions become finer and more sensitive, and his consciousness
becomes with time accustomed to the high tension of the divine force
flowing through him. His interior evolution proceeding, he invokes the
god of the *Sephirah* or plane immediately above. Following the same
procedure, he attempts to assimilate his own essence, his own
integrated consciousness, to that of the divinity he has invoked. And
so on — until finally he stands upon the lofty Darien peak of spiritual
realization, united with the transcendental life of infinity, feeling with
universal love and compassion, conscious of all life and every
thing as himself with supreme vision and power. As Iamblichus, the
Neoplatonic theurgist, once expressed it: 'If the essence and perfection
of all good are comprehended in the gods, and the first and ancient
power of them is with us priests [i.e. theurgists or magicians] and if by
those who similarly adhere to more excellent natures and genuinely
obtain a union with them, the beginning and end of all good is

earnestly pursued; if this be the case, here the contemplation of truth, and the possession of intellectual science are to be found. And a knowledge of the gods is accompanied with ... the knowledge of ourselves.'

So much for theory. How does the art of invocation proceed? Most important of all is the imaginative faculty. This must be trained to visualize symbols and images with the utmost clarity, ease, and precision. The necessity for this springs from the fact that certain god-forms are to be visualized. Most popular in magical techniques are the Egyptian god-forms. There seems to be a certain quality of specific definiteness about forms such as Osiris, Isis, Horus and Nuit, for example, which renders them peculiarly effective for this kind of training. In another system, where the archangels are synonymous with the divine gods, forms are visualized based upon an analysis of the individual letters comprising the God-name. That is to say, should we employ the Jewish Qabalistic system, each Hebrew letter has attributed to it a colour, astrological symbol, divinatory meaning in Tarot and Geomancy, and element. When building up the so-called telesmatic image of the archangel in the imagination, we take each letter as representing some particular part or limb of the form, and some particular shape, feature, or colour. Thus, from the letters of its name, a highly significant and eloquent form is ideally constructed.

Seated or lying in a perfectly relaxed physical state, one in which no muscular or nervous tension can send a disturbing message to the brain, the student endeavours to imagine that a particular god-form or telesmatic image surrounds him or coincides with his physical shape. Sometimes but a few minutes suffice to produce a conscious realization of the presence, though more often than not a good hour's work at the least is required to procure worthwhile results. As concentration and reflection become more intense and profound, the body becomes vitalized by streams of dynamic energy and power. The mind, too, is invaded by light, great intensity of feeling, and inspiration.

The name of the god or archangel is meanwhile frequently vibrated. This vibration serves two ends. One, to keep the mind well concentrated on the ideal form by means of repetition. Two, the vibration awakens in the depths of the microcosmic consciousness that magical faculty which is akin or corresponds to its macrocosmic power. Rhythmic breathing likewise is undertaken so as to tranquillize mind and body, and to open the subtler parts of the inner nature of the omni-present all-permeating life. Visualizations of the letters of the Name, moreover, are practised. According to traditional rules, the letters are manipulated by the mind as moving within the forms, or occupying certain important positions on plexuses or major nerve centres. The totality of these methods conspire to exalt the consciousness of the operator, to lift up his mind by no devious or uncertain route to a nobler interior plane where is a perception of the meaning and transcendental nature and being of the god.

Initiation

Over and above all these methods, or, more accurately, combining these techniques, is a final phase of Magic which I propose only to touch upon in brief – Initiation. The necessity and rationale of this process depends upon the postulated ability of a trained initiate to impart something of his own illumination and spiritual power to a candidate by means of a ceremony. Such a magnetic transmission of power is conceived to stir up the inner faculties of the candidate – faculties dormant and obscured for many a sorry year. As Psellus, another Neoplatonist once remarked of Magic, 'Its function is to initiate or perfect the human soul by the power of materials here on earth, for the supreme faculty of the soul cannot by its own guidance aspire to the sublimest intuitions, and to the comprehension of Divinity.'

Since the divine principles of man are obscured and latent within him, so that consciousness, of itself and by itself, is unable to climb to the distant heights of spiritual intimacy with universal life. Magic in the hands of a trained and experienced Magus is the means whereby that eclipse of the inner light may be overcome. By means of several initiations, the seeds of awakening are sown within the soul. Later they are fanned and stimulated into an active living flame lighting the brain, illuminating the soul, and providing the necessary guidance to accomplish the purpose of incarnation.

The number of ceremonies and their detailed implication must differ, naturally, with different systems, though, in general meaning, all are in complete accord. In one system of initiation, which is of especial significance to me personally, the major initiation ceremonies are seven in number. The first of these is a ceremony of preparation, consecration and purification, bringing to the dull gaze of the neophyte some vague intimation of the light to which he aspires and which seems lost in the dim darkness afar. The seed of the light is sown deeply within him by way of suggestions embodied in ritual speeches so that, time and devotion to the work acting as incubating agents, it may grow and blossom into the full-grown tree of illumination and divine union.

The next five ceremonies are concerned with developing what are termed the elemental bases of the soul. Consciousness, placed under the surveillance of the light, requires to be strengthened in its elemental aspects. So that when the light ultimately does dwell in the soul of man, the elemental self may be strong enough and pure enough to support the soul so that it may safely bear the full brunt of the divine glory. At first, this may not appear perhaps an urgent necessity. But if one remembers the pathologies of mysticism, the well-meaning but scatter-brained and unpractical people of this world who have been totally unfitted for the conquest of life by a mild species of psycho-spiritual experience, then the magical routine obtains some degree of justification. It is in vain that the wine of the gods is poured into old cracked vessels. We must make certain that the vessels are intact and strong, capable of retaining and not spilling the wine poured from above.

The five elemental ceremonies having been experienced, and the seeds of the divine earth, air, water, fire and ether sown within the human soul, the candidate is ready for the final initiation of this particular series. The central point of this initiation is the invocation of what commonly is called the higher self, or the Holy Guardian Angel. This is the central core of the individuality, the root of the unconscious. Before union with the Infinite may be envisaged, it is necessary that every principle in the human constitution be united so that man becomes one united consciousness, and not a disconnected series of separate discrete consciousnesses. The intelligence of the physical cells comprising the body, the principle of the emotions and feelings, the sphere of the mind itself, these must be united and bound together by a conscious realization of the true nature of the self employing them, the higher Genius. Integrity produced through the agency of the telestic or initiatory rites, then the whole human being, the entire man, may set forth upon that lengthy but incomparable bright road which leads to the end, and to the beginning also, of life. Then, and only then, is man able to realize the meaning of life, and the purpose of his multitudinous incarnations on earth. No longer is a vague mysticism countenanced and idealized as a cowardly escape from the difficulties and turmoils of this life. With these latter he is now capable of dealing and, moreover, of completely mastering them, so that no longer do they enslave him. By no ties, either of attachment or disgust, is he bound to the duties of this earth – ties which must necessitate his further and continued incarnation until he has successfully severed them.

Freedom obtained through the acquisition of integrity in its truest and divinest sense, then the next magical step in evolution is possible of recognition and achievement – the conscious return of man to the divine Light from which he came.

3. The Meaning of Magic

We live today in a world of great material progress and mechanical ingenuity. On every hand are flouted the social advantages of the world-wide communication bequeathed to us by such modern inventions as aviation, radio and space craft. Time seems to disappear in the face of such things, and space dwindles almost to nothing. The peoples of the earth are drawn far closer together than ever they have been before in recorded history. By way of paradox, however, simultaneously with this unique advance in scientific progress, a large proportion of mankind is supremely miserable. It suffers the pangs of dire starvation because scientific methods have yielded an over-production of foods and manufactured articles without having solved the problem of distribution. Yet modern science has become invested with a nature which originally was not its own. Despite the chaos of international affairs, and the fear of another catastrophic war present in the minds of most people, it has become robed in a mighty grandeur, almost of divinity.

Perhaps it is because of this feeling of insecurity and fear that this condition has come about, for the human psyche is a cowardly thing at core. We cannot bear to be honest with ourselves, accepting the idea that whilst we are human we are bound to feel insecurity, anxiety and inferiority. Instead, we project these fears outwards upon life, and invest science, or any body of knowledge, with a vast potential of effect so as to bolster up our dwindling fund of courage. So science has become, thanks to our projection, an authority that hardly dares to be questioned. We cannot bear that it *should* be questioned for we must feel that in this subject at least is authority, unshakeable knowledge and the security we so dearly crave. The phenomenon is hardly dissimilar to that of a few centuries ago when religion, formal religion of the churches, was the recipient of this obeisance and respect. For many people, science has now become their intellectual keynote, by whose measuring rod – despite their own personal neuroses and moral defects – all things are ruled, accepted or rejected.

Science and Magic

Pursuits, no matter of what nature, that temporarily are not popularly favoured, even though in them lies the hope for the spiritual advancement of the world, or subjects that do not possess the sanction of those who are the leading lights in the scientific world, are apt to receive as their lot neglect and gross misunderstanding. When many folk are introduced to Magic, for instance, the first reaction is either one of stark fear and horror – or else we are greeted by a smile of the utmost condescension. This is followed by the retort, intended to be devastating, that Magic is synonymous with superstition, that its tenets were long ago exploded, and that, moreover, it is unscientific. This, I believe, is the experience of the majority of people whose prime interest is Magic or what now passes as occultism. It seems that, just as their hope for security and their desire for unshakeable knowledge becomes projected upon science, so their inner fears and unfaced terrors are projected upon this maltreated body of traditional knowledge, Magic. Disconcerting this reaction can most certainly be, unless criticism and the call for definitions is immediately resorted to. By these means alone may we who champion Magic obtain a begrudged hearing.

Science is a word meaning knowledge. Hence any body of knowledge, regardless of its character – whether ancient, mediaeval, or modern – is a science. Technically, however, the word is reserved primarily to imply that kind of knowledge that has been reduced to systematic order. This order is encompassed by means of accurate observation experimentally carried out over a period of time, the classification of the behaviour of natural phenomena alone, and the deduction of general laws to explain and to account for that behaviour. If this be the case, then Magic must likewise claim inclusion within the scope of the same term. For the content of Magic has been observed, recorded and described in no uncertain terms over a great period of time. And though its phenomena are other than physical, being almost exclusively psychological in their effect, they are, of course, natural. General laws, too, have been evolved to account for and to explain its phenomena.

Definitions of Magic

A definition of Magic presents a rather more difficult task. A short definition which will really explain its nature and describe the field of its operation seems practically impossible. One dictionary defines it as 'the art of applying natural causes to produce surprising effects.' Havelock Ellis has ventured the sugestion that a magical act is a name which may well be given to cover every conceivable act in the whole of life's span. It is Aleister Crowley's suggestion that 'Magic is the science and art of causing changes to occur in conformity with will.' Dion Fortune slightly modified this by adding a couple of words – 'changes in consciousness'. The anonymous mediaeval author of *The Goetia, or Lesser Key of King Solomon* has written a proem to that book where occurs the passage that states, 'Magic is the highest, most absolute, and most divine knowledge of Natural philosophy ... True àgents being applied to proper patients strange and admirable effects will thereby be produced. Whence magicians are profound and diligent searchers into Nature.'

Have these definitions taught us anything of a precise nature about the subject? Personally, I doubt it very much; all are too general in their scope to tend towards edification. Let us therefore cease seeking definitions and consider first of all certain aspects or fundamental principles of the subject. Afterwards, perhaps, we may have sufficient trustworthy and evidential material at our disposal to formulate anew a definition which may convey something intelligible and precise to our minds.

Within the significance of the one term 'Magic' are comprehended several quite independent techniques. It may be advantageous to examine some of these techniques. Before doing so, however, it might be well to consider a part of the underlying theory. I know many will say by way of criticism of this discussion, that it is nothing but primitive psychology – and only the psychology of auto-suggestion at that. There will be a decided sneer, barely concealed.

However, this objection does not completely dispose of the subject by any means. A very great deal more remains to be said. Not that I would deny that in Magic the process of self-suggestion is absent. Most certainly it is present. But what I must emphasize here is the fact that it is present in a highly evolved and elaborate form. It almost makes the technical approach of some of our modern experimenters look puerile and undeveloped. We are not to suppose for one moment that the innovators and developers of the magical processes in days gone by were naive or fools, unaware of human psychology and the structure of the mind itself, nor that they refrained from facing many of the psychic problems with which we nowadays have had to deal. Many of the early magicians were wise and skilled men, artists and sages, well-versed in the ways and means of influencing and affecting people.

We know that they understood a good deal about hypnotism and the induction of hypnoidal states. It is highly probable that they speculated, as have done innumerable modern psychologists, upon technical methods of inducing hypnoidal states without the aid and help of a second person. But they soon became aware of all the obstacles and barriers that beset their path. And these were many. I believe that in Magic they devised a highly efficient technical procedure for overcoming these difficulties.

The Unconscious

When Coué some years ago burst upon our startled horizon with his spectacular formula of 'day by day in every way I am getting better and better', many believed that here at last we were presented with the ideal method of getting down to brass tacks, of finally being able to impinge upon the unconscious mind, so called. Hundreds of thousands of people surely must have gone to bed at night, determined to induce a relaxation that was as nearly perfect as they could obtain, and attempted to enter the land of slumber while muttering sleepily the magical formula over and over again. Others listened to music in dimly lighted rooms until they experienced some sense of exaltation and then mumbled the healing phrase until they felt that surely some favourable result must occur.

Assuredly some lucky people got results. They were, however, few and far between. Some of these did overcome certain physical handicaps of illness, nervousness, so-called defects in speech and other mannerisms, and thus were able to better themselves and their positions in the world of reality. Others were less fortunate – and these were by far the greater number, the great majority.

What was the difficulty that prevented these people, this large majority, from applying the magical formula until success was theirs? Why were they not able to penetrate that veil stretched between the various levels of their minds?

Before we answer these questions – and I believe that Magic does really answer them – let us analyze the situation a little more closely.

The unconscious in these systems of so-called practical psychology, metaphysics, and auto-suggestion, is considered a slumbering giant. These systems hold that it is a veritable storehouse of power and energy. It controls every function of the body every moment of every day, nor does it sleep or tire. The heart beats seventy-two times per minute, and every three or four seconds our lungs will breathe in oxygen and exhale carbonic acid and other waste products. The intricate and complex process of digestion and assimilation of food which becomes part and parcel of our very being, the circulation of blood, the growth, development and multiplication of cells, the organic resistance to infection – all these processes are conceived of as immediately under the control of this portion of our minds of which we are not normally aware – the unconscious.

This is only one theoretical approach to the unconscious. There are other definitions of its nature and function which altogether preclude the practical possibility of resorting to suggestion or auto-suggestion for coping with our ills. For example, there is the definition provided by Jung with which in many ways I am in sympathy, and it might be worth our while to quote it at some length. He wrote in *Modern Man in Search of a Soul* that,

> Man's unconscious likewise contains all the patterns of life and behaviour inherited from his ancestors, so that every human child, prior to consciousness, is possessed of a potential system of adapting psychic functioning ... While consciousness is intensive and concentrated, it is transient and is directed upon the immediate present and the immediate field of attention; moreover, it has access only to material that represents one individual's experience stretching over a few decades ... But matters stand very differently with the unconscious. It is not concentrated and intensive, but shades off into obscurity; it is highly extensive and can juxtapose the most heterogeneous elements in the most paradoxical way. More than this, it contains besides an indeterminable number of subliminal perceptions, an immense fund of accumulated inheritance-factors left by one generation of men after another, whose mere existence marks a step in the differentiation of the species. If it were permissible to personify the unconscious, we might call it a collective human being combining the characteristics of both sexes, transcending youth and age, birth and death, and, from having at his command a human experience of one or two million years, almost immortal. If such a being existed, he would be exalted above all temporal change; the present would mean neither more or less to him than any year in the one hundredth century before Christ; he would be a dreamer of age-old dreams and, owing to his immeasurable experience, he would be an incomparable prognosticator. He would have lived countless times over the life of the individual, of the family, tribe and people, and he would possess the living sense of the rhythm of growth, flowering and decay.

Granted this kind of definition, the whole idea of suggesting ideas to this 'dreamer of age-old dreams', sounds utterly presumptuous. Only a simpleton, living a superficial intellectual and spiritual life, would have the audacity to dare give this 'being' suggestions relative to business, marriage, or health. Such a concept, then, immediately rules out the use of suggestion, demanding more sophisticated approaches.

The Endopsychic Barrier

For the time being, and only for the purpose of this discussion, let us grant validity to the first concept of the unconscious as being a titan who may respond to suggestions. The theory goes, therefore, that if, in the face of some bodily ill or disfunction, we could literally *tell* the unconscious what we want done, these results could occur in answer to our concentrated wish. Theoretically, the theory sounds all right. Unfortunately, for one thing, it does not take into consideration the fact that early in life an impenetrable barrier is erected within the psyche itself; a barrier of inhibition is built up between the unconscious and the conscious thinking self – a barrier of prejudices, false moral concepts, infantile notions, pride and egotism. So profound is this armoured barrier that our best attempts to get past it, around it, or through it are utterly impotent. We become cut off from our roots, and have no power, no ability, to contact the deeper, the instinctual, the more potent side of our natures.

The various schools of auto-suggestion and metaphysics all have different theories and techniques with regard to overcoming this barrier. That some people do succeed is unquestionable. One meets almost every day an individual here and there who is able to 'demonstrate' – to use the ghastly word they so glibly employ. These few are able to impress their unconscious minds with certain ideas which fall as though upon fertile soil, fructify and bring salutary results. These we cannot deny – much as sometimes we would like to, so offensive is their smugness, their dogmatic attitude, their unthinkingness.

But by far the great majority of their devotees fail lamentably. They have not, obviously, been able to overcome this difficulty by the employment of the usual routines.

I am sure the ancient sages and magi knew of these problems – knew them very well. I am also quite sure that they realized that the technique they used was, amongst other things, a process of suggesting a series of creative ideas to themselves. But what I am equally certain of is this: they had perfected an almost ideal method which proved itself able to penetrate this hitherto impenetrable endopsychic barrier. They were able to reach this imprisoned titan locked up in the hearts of every one of us, and set it free so that it could work with them and for them. Thus they became almost lyrical in their descriptions of what could not be accomplished by the individual who employed their techniques with courage and perseverance.

As I say, they knew of the existence of this psychic armour, and knew it only too well. All their methods were directed to mobilizing all the forces of the individual, reinforcing his will and imagination, to the end that he could overcome himself to realize his kinship, his identity and unity with the unconscious self.

What these methods were, I hope to describe in some small detail in these pages. Some of them may appear irrational to us. They certainly are irrational. But that is no argument for rejecting them summarily. A great part of life itself is irrational. But it is incumbent upon us to accept life in all its aspects, rational and irrational as well. One of the very earliest things a psychoanalytic patient learns is this one fact – that he has at least two sides to his nature, a rational and an irrational side. Together they comprise a single discrete self – his personality. If he denies the validity or existence of either one of them, he does violence to himself and must suffer accordingly. Both of these two factors must be permitted to exist side by side, the one affecting the other. In this way, the individual grows, intellectually, emotionally and spiritually, and all his ways will prosper. With denial, nothing but trouble, neurosis and disease can follow.

These irrational processes that were instituted of old as the technique of Magic comprise the use of invocation or prayer, of the use of the imagination in formulating images and symbols, of employing the religious sense to awaken ecstasy and an intensity of feeling, of rates of breathing that would alter the accustomed neuro-physiological patterns and so render more permeable the barrier within the mind itself. Everything that would conduce to a heightening of feeling and imagination, that would lead to the instigation of an overpowering ecstasy, would be encouraged, for it would be in this psychological state that the normal barriers and confines of the conscious personality could be overridden in a tempestuous storm of emotional concentration.

Concentration and Emotion

It was the ancient theory that the unconscious or the deeper levels of the psyche could be reached principally by two methods. These were intense concentration, and intensity of emotion. The former is extremely difficult of achievement. Certainly there are methods whereby the mind itself may be trained so to concentrate that eventually a funnel, as it were, is created by the mind, through which suggestions could be poured into the unconscious to work their way out in the various ways desired. But such methods are for the very few. There is only an individual here and there who has the patience and the indomitable will to sit by himself for a certain period during the day, and each day, and subject himself to an iron mental discipline.

The emotional intensity, while not easy to cultivate, at least is more within the bounds and possibilities of achievement than is the other. It was this method that the ancient magicians cultivated to a very fine art. They devised innumerable means whereby the normal physio-logical habits could be changed and altered, so as to permit of this impingement upon the underlying basis of the self.

To summarize: there is divination, the art of obtaining at a moment's notice any required type of information regarding the outcome of certain actions or events. Fortune-telling so-called is an abuse. The sole purpose of the art is to develop the intuitive faculties of the student to such an extent that eventually all technical methods of divination may be discarded. When that stage of development has been reached, mere reflection upon any problem will automatically evoke from the intuitive mechanism within the information required, with a degree of certainty and assurance involved that could never be acquired save from an inner psychic source.

Another phase – perhaps which has been stressed more than all others – is Ceremonial Magic in its widest sense. Comprised within this expression, are at least three distinct types of ceremonial endeavour, all, however, subject to one general set of rules or governed by one major formula. The word 'ceremonial' includes rituals for initiation, for the invocation of gods so-called, and the evocation of elemental and planetary spirits. There is also the enormous sphere of talismans, and their consecration and charging. Ceremonial is probably the most ideal of all methods for spiritual development since it entails the analysis and subsequent stimulation of every individual faculty and power. Its results are genius and spiritual illumination. But personal aptitude is so potent a factor in this matter, as well as in divination, that although the word 'Art' may be applied to cover their operation it would be unjust to Magic to denominate it a Science.

The third, and in some ways the most important branch for my particular purpose at the moment, is vision, or the Body of Light technique. It is with this latter that I shall deal exclusively in this essay, as it contains elements which I feel answer more definitely to the requirements of a Science than any other.

Magic and the Qabalah

In discussing Magic, the reader's pardon must be sought if reference is continually made to the Qabalah. They are so interlaced that it is well-nigh impossible to separate them. Qabalah is theory and philosophy. On the other hand, Magic is the practical application of that theory. In the Qabalah is a geometrical glyph named The Tree of Life, which is really a symbolic map both of the universe in its major aspects, and of its microcosm, man. Upon this map are depicted ten principal continents, so to say, or ten fields of activity where the forces constituting or underlying the universe function in their respective ways. In man these are analysable into ten facets of consciousness, ten modes of spiritual activity. These are called the *Sephiroth* (see page 57).

Now consider with me that especial *Sephirah* or subtle aspect of the universe called by the Qabalists *Yesod*. Translated as the 'sphere of the Foundation', it is part of the Astral Light – an omniform plane of magnetic, electric, and ubiquitous substance, interpenetrating and underlying the whole of the visible perceptible world. It acts as a more or less permanent mould whereupon the physical world is constructed, its own activity and constant change ensuring the stability of this world as a compensating factor. In this world function the dynamics of feeling, desire and emotion, and just as the activities of this physical world are engineered through the modalities of heat and cold, compression and diffusion, etc., so in the astral are operative attraction and repulsion, love and hate.

Another of its functions is to exist as the memory of nature, where are automatically and instantaneously recorded every act of man and every phenomenon of the universe from time immemorial to the present day. The nineteenth-century Magus, Eliphas Lévi, has written of this Astral Light that: 'There exists an agent which is natural and divine, material and spiritual, a universal plastic mediator, a common receptacle of the vibrations of motion and the images of forms, a fluid and a force, which may be called in some way the Imagination of Nature ...' And again he registers the conviction that it is 'the mysterious force whose equilibrium is social life, progress, civilization, and whose disturbance is anarchy, revolution, barbarism, from whose chaos a new equilibrium at length evolves, the cosmos of a new order, when another dove has brooded over the blackened and disturbed waters.'

The Astral Light and the Collective Unconscious

It is interesting to glance from this theurgic concept to a psychological one which is not very unlike it. The following paragraph is more or less of a paraphrase of Jung's ideas concerning it, culled from an essay of his entitled *Analytical Psychology and Weltanschauung*. It is an extension of the ideas previously quoted. He defines it first of all as the all-controlling deposit of ancestral experience from untold millions of years, the echo of prehistoric world-events to which each century adds an infinitesimally small amount of variation and differentiation. Because it is in the last analysis a deposit of world-events finding expression in brain and sympathetic nerve structure, it becomes, in its totality, a sort of timeless world-image, with a certain aspect of eternity opposed to our momentary, conscious image of the world. It has an energy peculiar to itself, independent of consciousness, by means of which effects are produced in the psyche that influence us all the more powerfully from the dark regions within. These influences remain invisible to everyone who has failed to subject the transient world-image to adequate criticism, and who is therefore still hidden from himself. That the world has not only an outer, but an inner aspect, and that it is not only outwardly visible, but also acts powerfully upon us in a timeless present, from the deepest and most subjective hinterland of the psyche – this Jung holds to be a form of knowledge that, regardless of the fact that it is ancient wisdom, deserves to be evaluated as a new factor in forming a philosphic world-view. I suggest, then, that what the magicians imply by the Astral Light is identical in the last resort with the Collective Unconscious of modern psychology.

By means of the traditional theurgic technique it is possible to contact consciously this plane, to experience its life and influence, converse with its elemental and angelic inhabitants so-called, and return here to normal consciousness with complete awareness and memory of that experience. This, naturally requires training. But so does every department of science. Intensive preparation is demanded to fit one for critical observation, to provide one with the particular scientific alphabet required for its study, and to acquaint one with the researches of one's predecessors in that realm. No less should be expected of Magic – though all too often miracles are expected without due preparation. Anyone with even the slightest visual imagination may be so trained as to handle in but a short while the elementary magical technique by which one is enabled to explore the subtler aspects of life and the universe. To transcend this 'many-coloured world' and to gain admittance to loftier realms of soul and spirit is quite another matter, one calling for other faculties and other powers, particularly a fiery devotion and an intense aspiration to the highest.

But with the latter, I am not just now concerned, even though it is the pulsing heart and more important aspect of Theurgy. It is with the scientific aspect of Magic, its more readily verifiable aspect, that I shall deal now. Elsewhere I have given as traditional attributions or associations to the sphere in question the following symbols. Its planet is said to be the moon, its element air, its number nine, its colour purple – and also silver in another scale. The pearl and moonstone are its jewels, aloes its perfume, and its so-called divine name is *Shaddai El Chai*. The archangel attributed to it is Gabriel, its choir of angels are the four Kerubs ruling the elements, and its geomantic symbols are Populus and Via. The Tarot symbols appertaining to this sphere are those cards in each of the four suits numbered IX, and closely associated with it also is the twenty-first trump card entitled 'The

World'. Here we find depicted a female form surrounded by a green garland. Actually this trump card is attributed to the thirty-second path of Saturn which connects the material plain to *Yesod*. But how were these symbols and names obtained? What is their origin? And why are they so called attributions or correspondences of that *Sephirah* called the Foundation?

First of all, meditation will disclose the fact that all have a natural harmony and affinity one with the other – though not perhaps readily seen at the first glance. For example, the moon is, to us, the fastest moving planet. It travels through all the twelve signs of the zodiac in about twenty-eight days. The idea of rapid change is there implicit, revealing the concept that the astral, while almost a timeless eternal deposit of world events, is nevertheless the origin of mutations and alterations which later influence the physical world – in the same way that impulse and thought must precede any action. Its element is air, a subtle, all-pervading medium, comparable to the astral light itself – a medium without which life is quite impossible. Nine is the end of all numbers, containing the preceding numbers within its own sum. It always remains itself when added to itself or multiplied, or subtracted, suggesting the fundamental, all-inclusive, self-sustaining nature of the realm.

What is still more important, however, from the scientific viewpoint, is that they are things, names, and symbols actually perceived in that sphere by the skryer in the spirit-vision. As a matter of solid proof, one could quote numerous visions and astral journeys obtained by different people in difference places at different times, in which all the traditional symbols apear in dynamic and in curiously dramatic and vital form.

Experimental Verification

Magic, as already remarked, is a practical system, and every part has been devised for experiment. Each part is capable of verification using appropriate methods. Each student may check it for himself, and thus discover the realities of his own divine nature as well as of the universe both within and without him, independently of what any other man may have written in books. We ask for experiment; demand it even, for the sake of mankind. We invite the earnest and sincere student to experiment for himself with that technique described in Chapter Ten of my book *The Tree of Life*, and then compare his results, the journey to any one path or *Sephirah*, with the correspondences briefly delineated in my other work *A Garden of Pomegranates* or in Dion Fortune's book *The Mystical Qabalah*. It is with the utmost confidence that I say one hundred astral journeys obtained in that way will correspond in *every* instance with the major symbols, names, numbers, and ideas recorded in the several books of the Qabalah.

Let me quote from the record of a colleague an illuminating passage or two illustrating what I mean. The following is a 'vision' or waking dream – a fantasy of the so-called thirty-second path.

> We marched down the wide indigo road. There was a cloudy night-sky – no stars. The road was raised above the general level of the ground. There was a canal each side beyond which we could see the lights of what appeared to be a large city. We went on like this for a long way, but then I noticed in the distance a tiny figure of a woman, like a miniature – she seemed to be naked, but as she drew near, I saw a scarf floating round her. She had a crown of stars on her head and in her hands were two wands. She came towards us very quickly, and I gazed fascinatedly at a string of pearls reaching from her neck to her knees – and gazing, found that we had passed through the circle of pearls, and she had disappeared!

The student of the Qabalah who has only a passing acquaintance with Tarot symbolism will recognize here the twenty-first Atu of 'The World', the path attributed to Saturn, linking the physical to the astral worlds. He will probably be very surprised to learn that the symbols on these cards represent dynamic and exceedingly vital realities. But I must pass on to a brief description of the entrance to *Yesod*.

> Now the sky is clear and full of stars ... the moon, a great yellow harvest moon, rises slowly up the sky to a full arch ... and we saw the moonbeams shining on the high purple walls of a city ... We did not delay to look about, but marched quickly to the centre of the city, to an open space, in the midst of which was a round temple like a ball of silver. It was approached by nine steps, and rested on a silver platform. It had four doors. Before each was a large angel with silver wings ... Inside, we were in a very airy place. Light breezes lifted our clothes and our hair – the interior was very white and clear silvery – no colours. Suspended in the centre was a great globe, like the moon itself ... While we looked we saw that the globe was not suspended in the air; it rested on immense cupped hands. We followed the arms up and saw, far up near the roof, deep dark eyes looking down, dark like the night sky. And a voice said ...

Little point would be gained in continuing with the rest of the quotation. This passage is given here solely that the reader may refer to the description of the astral plane in the textbooks, and then to the recurrence in this vision of the major symbols, and the dynamic form of dramatization. Let the student take good notice of the presence of the correct numbers, colours, planetary attributions, and above all the hint as to how much valuable knowledge may be acquired. Note the four doors to the temple – representing the four major elements of fire, water, air and earth. For this astral world is also referred to as the ether (of which the element air is a surrogate), the fifth element quintessentializing the lower elements, the temple to which the other elements are but doors.

Suspended in the centre of the temple was a globe, symbolic possibly of the element air itself which, in the Hindu Tattwa system, is represented by a blue sphere. Before each of the doors stands an angel. These are the four Kerubic angels, the vice-regents of the four cardinal quarters and elements ruling over a particular elemental world under the dominance of one of the letters of the Tetragrammaton. Possibly they are representations of the interior psychic delimitation of the soul's spatial area, so to speak, the absence of which would indicate an unhealthy diffusion or decentralization of consciousness. Also the four cardinal points of space would be represented by these four angelic figures – concretizations, too, of the double play of the moral opposites. East is opposite to west, and north opposite to south, whilst each of these quarters has attributed to it some particular moral quality or psychic function. The sense of being in an airy place with light breezes bears out the formal attribution of air – a curious confirmation of the duality of meaning implied in *pneuma*, wind and spirit, a duality which occurs not only in the Greek, but in Hebrew, Arabic, and a host of primitive languages.

The Reality of Magic

Individual after individual has been trained independently to visit this and other *Sephiroth*. While each vision is somewhat different in its detail and form to that here quoted, nevertheless there is a startling unanimity so far as concerns the essential symbolic features. This constitutes definite scientific proof of the supreme reality of the world of Magic, and demonstrates the possibility of personal experiment and research. Scientific research is possible in this world of astral or unconscious realities, because they are effective things, that is, objective influences that work and influence mankind. This sphere is the deposit of the world experience of all times, and it is therefore an image of the world that has been forming for aeons, an image in which certain features, the so-called dominants, have been elaborated through the course of time. These dominants are the ruling powers, the gods and archangels and angels – that is, represenations of dominating laws and principles functioning in the cosmos. And since it is a world functioning in the brain structure and sympathetic nervous system of every individual it is a world which is open to every one who wishes to overcome the fear which centuries of mal-education have projected upon it, and discover for himself anew the reality of its dynamic urges and influences.

With but little ingenuity, specific tests may be undertaken with the object of testing the relationship between geometrical symbols, the vision obtained therefrom by means of the body of light technique, and the correspondences of these figures recorded in the proper books. It has been written that various elements – fire, water, spirit, air and earth – are attributed to the five points of the Pentagram. Depending entirely on the direction in which the lines are traced, so will the figure invoke or banish the beings pertaining to that element. For example, if the student traces the invoking Pentagram of Fire in each of the four cardinal quarters, and then employs the sensitive sight of the Body of Light which previously he has cultivated, he will see appear almost immediately the fire elementals or Salamanders, the personalized fiery constituents of his own psyche. The tracing of the banishing Fire Pentagram will see them literally scuttle away without hesitation, subsiding into the unconscious realm to which they belong, and from which they were called.

Or else let the student do this experiment in the presence of a reliable clairvoyant, not mentioning what figure is being traced. The results will be highly illuminating. I know some objection may be raised by immediately responding 'telepathy'. But so far as I can see, the response arouses far more obscure problems than the rationale to which objection is made; for telepathy certainly requires explanation along scientific and dependable lines – quite difficult at this stage of the game. These and a host of other rigorous tests constitute definite and precise scientific experiment of a significant and highly authoritative nature.

In the sense that several people may travel to certain paths and there undergo experiences wherein the essential features are identical or in which the psychic dominants coincide, Magic may be assumed to be a definite, coherent science. It is precise and accurate. Magic is the accumulated record of psychic and spiritual experience which we have inherited from the past, from former generations of mankind.

On the other hand, it is clear that each of these visions would differ materially as to context, that is, in the dramatic sense. The context, act and scene so to speak, depend, entirely upon personal idiosyncrasy, intellectual integrity, and the spiritual capacity to discover and absorb the truth, whether it is painful to the ego or not. Where the personal element enters so powerfully as it does here, the adventure must be labelled an art. Creative imagination in one person will be used to formulate with an established conventional set of symbols a whole string of incidents and experiences – illuminating and tending to the expansion of his consciousness – which to the vision of a simple unimaginative person would occur in far simpler and matter-of-fact form.

Sophisticated people, with a smattering of modern psychology, are likely to assume that Magic discloses nothing but the hidden depths of the unconscious. They will say that these journeys are comparable to dream experiences which are referred to the working and dramatizing power of the subconscious mind. What difference does it make if the Qabalists named this sphere or type of consciousness the Foundation or Astral World and the moderns 'the unconscious'?The terms are cognate, and the symbols interchangeable; both mean the same thing, when all things are considered. If magic possesses weapons that are more penetrating and incisive than scientific ones, shall we reject them because magic is the discredited house wherein they are stored? If magical methods reveal our secret selves more directly, and unlock the vast store of wisdom and power within our souls, showing us how to control them in ways that neither psycho-analysis nor any modern science has succeeded to do, should we not be foolish to rejects its benefits?

Magic is a scientific method. It is a valid technique. Its approach to the universe and to the secret of life's meaning is a legitimate one. If it assists us to become more familiar with what we *really* are, it is a science – and a most important one. And to the scientist, whether he be psychologist or physicist, it will open up an entirely new universe of tremendous breadth and depth. If it succeeds in making us better men and women, a little more kind and generous, a little more aware of the spiritual heights to which we are capable of climbing with but a little exertion, then it is the religion of religions. And should it spur us to greater efforts in order to render life and living more beautiful and intelligible, should it make us more anxious to eliminate ugliness, suffering, and ignoble misery, surely it is an art before which all other Muses must bow the head and bend the knee in reverential and perennial praise!

2. A QABALISTIC PRIMER

A Layman's Guide to The Tree of Life

The Qabalah is an archaic system of Jewish mysticism. S.L. MacGregor Mathers in his learned introduction on this subject wrote many years ago that the principal doctrines of the Qabalah were designed to solve the following problems:

1. The Supreme Being, His nature and attributes.
2. Cosmogony.
3. The creation of angels and man.
4. The destiny of man and angels.
5. The nature of the soul.
6. The nature of angels, demons, and elementals.
7. The import of the revealed law.
8. The transcendental symbolism of numerals.
9. The peculiar mysteries contained in the Hebrew letters.
10. The equilibrium of contraries.

Christian Ginsburg, LL.D., a hostile critic of some fifty years ago, wished to differentiate between Jewish mysticism on the one hand and the Qabalah on the other. His unsympathetic attitude was predicated on the narrowness of so-called nineteenth-century rationalism. This attitude has since been discarded in the sciences as it has been in the study of mysticism.

That Ginsburg's intransigent point of view is no longer valid is strongly stressed by one of the most incisive of all modern Hebraic scholars, Gershom G. Scholem. In his masterful work, *The Kaballah and its Symbolism*, he states simply that the Qabalah literally means 'tradition'. As such, it is the tradition of divine things, an esoteric tradition. Thus, it is the sum of Jewish mysticism.

He proceeds further by adding that it has had a long history, far longer and more stable than has hitherto been suspected. For centuries it has exerted a profound religious and philosophical influence on those of the Jewish people who were desirous of deepening their understanding of the more prosaic or orthodox forms and conceptions of Judaism. For him and many other scholars like him, therefore, Ginsburg's criticism is entirely without meaning, not being rooted in historical fact.

Commentaries and Translations

The Qabalah is not a particular book, as some laymen have erroneously assumed. It is a literature − a vast literature, much of it belonging to the Middle Ages and some to earlier Gnostic periods. Most of it still remains in Hebrew and Aramaic. During the mystical renaissance in the eighteenth century in Poland and central Europe, the Chassidic period, the literature underwent expansion, reinterpretation and republication. Some little of this had been translated into German. Rather less of it had appeared in English. A great deal still requires to be rendered into English in order to round out our wholly inadequate knowledge.

Only a few of its major classics are currently available. For example, the *Zohar*, which was translated by Sperling and Simon, was originally published in the 1930s by the Soncino Press in England. The much smaller *Sepher Yetzirah* has long been obtainable in several different translations. Its miniscule size made it a less formidable task of translation than did the *Zohar*.

Some few commentaries and books about different aspects of this literature have been translated or written in English. A great part of this latter material, interestingly enough, has been done by non-Jews who are mystics and occult students. Having found the Qabalah useful and interesting, they did not, however, try to use it as a technical device to convert the people of Israel wholesale to Christ − as has been attempted before. A good part of this more recent work, listed at the end of this essay, has been on a very high level, both from a literary and a didactic point of view, and is likely to survive for quite a long time.

As a Jewish mysticism, the Qabalah is naturally very Jewish. Some books of the Qabalah not only elaborate theories and sectarian explanations based on early Rabbinical exegesis of Old Testament texts and Hebrew belief and history, but differ from most other systems of mysticism by extensive elaboration of the 'chosen people' theme, elevating it into a sort of cosmically determined fact.

This approach may not necessarily be very appealing to many of us today, Christian or Jew. We feel little need for the formal context and content of institutionalized religion of any sect or denomination.

The Tree of Life

The fundamental basis of the Qabalah from the modern point of view rests not on its mysticial speculations about creation, eschatology, the Messiah, the Sabbath, and so on – but on 'The Tree of Life'. This is a simple theoretical and mathematical structure based on a 'filing cabinet' idea.

This essentially illuminating possibility was really laid down in *The Sepher Yetzirah*. Here certain ideas are systematically attributed to the basic system of numbers from one to ten. Furthermore, each of the twenty-two letters of the Hebrew alphabet are elaborated in much the same way – an idea quite intelligible when it is remembered that the Hebrew letters are, at the same time, numbers. The sum total of the ten numerals and the twenty-two letters comprise the thirty-two Paths of Wisdom, as they are called, and represent 'The Tree of Life'.

To each one of these Paths, this early *Book of Formation* attributes planets, zodiacal signs, divine names, elements, directions in space, etc. This is done in such a manner as to formulate the rudiments of a filing system. Later generations of scholars and students, by using this root system, have added a complex series of additional data. This includes information from Greek and Egyptian mythology, meditative material derived from the Tarot, information based on mystical experience (visionary and ecstatic), a conglomerate of sounds and smells and colours – perfumes, jewels and, significantly too, modern scientific data. It has become a meaningful syncretism.

The Organization of Knowledge

The whole *mélange* thus serves as a further means of classifying all knowledge. It serves to organize the contents of the mind and to provide a mechanism for unifying all systems of any and every kind. Thus, ultimately, it enables one to reduce all types and kinds of knowledge to unity. And so we return to the heart, not simply of the Jewish Qabalah, but of all mysticism: 'For I have found Thee alike in the Me and the Thee; there is no difference, O my beautiful, my desirable One! In the One and the Many have I found Thee: yea, I have found Thee.'

Once the potentiality of this root idea is grasped, it can be seen as infinitely more important, significant and useful than any quasi-mystical theory of cosmogensis or anthropogenesis. It is far more productive and vastly more creative than esoteric hypotheses as to why the Jews were selected as the chosen people, what went on in heaven during the Exile, or how the Messiah weeps on high on learning of the privations and sorrows of the dispersed people of Israel. Any archaic psychology or Christology or theology fades into minor importance when it is placed on the Tree and perceived in relation to other data from similar esoteric systems.

The subject of the Qabalah is so vast that in order to manage it more intelligently an arbitrary division of its content material should be made into four specific segments. We must remember at all times, however, that the division is wholly arbitrary and for our convenience only. Each section is really without any dividing line, spilling over and spreading into every other section.

1. *Comparative.* By using the Tree of Life as a mathematical structure, a science of comparative religion and mysticism is brought within the bounds of possibility. It can be employed to heighten understanding by relating one set of known concepts to others in a far different and distant system, thus reducing the many to the One. This essay is concerned solely with an elementary introduction to this theme.

2. *Doctrinal.* This consists of a mystico-theological exposition of some of the great problems that have always preoccupied mankind. The traditional Qabalah has its own unique points of view. I doubt, however, that it has too much validity in today's world. Nevertheless, it is a distinct attitude, and as such is to be respected and compared to other esoteric systems.

3. *Theurgic.* This has also been called the magical or wonder-working tradition of the Qabalah. It is strongly rooted in the esoteric traditions relating to The Tree of Life, which has its roots in the divine, secret life of God. In effect, the entire theory and practice revolve around the 'way of return' to the Godhead from which man has become alienated. The more modern interpretations of technical procedures and methodology are vastly different from and superior to the more ancient and specifically Jewish point of view. It is in effect a more universal, eclectic approach rooted in that curious phenomenon of the last century, the genius of the Hermetic Order of the Golden Dawn.

4. *Exegetical.* Some contemporaries who know no Hebrew, and who have received no schooling or discipline in these aspects of the Qabalah, have written foolishly that these methods are unimportant. This is to be understood as merely a frank confession of their own lack of experience and understanding. The tyro who has developed

even minor facility in the use of these techniques or exegesis opens himself to fantastic insights which, in their own way, are relevant mystical experiences.

It is this latter, the realization of the universe as being divine, the entire body of God which includes every man and every form of life within its vastness, which is the goal of *all* mysticism. If this technical approach can yield this ultimate goal, its employment is not to be sneered at or minimized.

The Ten Sephiroth

The oustanding feature of The Tree of Life once we begin to examine it closely, is revealed as a system of the ten *Sephiroth* or divine emanations, divided into three columns. There is a right and a left column of three *Sephiroth* each, and a middle one of four. The right one is called the Pillar of Mercy; the left, the Pillar of Severity – the prototypes of the Masonic pillars of *Yachin* and *Boaz*. One of these is male, the other female; one is positive, the other negative. One is white, the other is black. And so on – the eternal play of the opposites: 'Remember that unbalanced force is evil, that unbalanced severity is but cruelty and oppression, but that also unbalanced mercy is but weakness which would allow and abet evil.'

Thus the Qabalah stresses a middle way between the two opposites, indicating the age-old need for the avoidance of extremes. This attitude is also found in Hindu philosophy, in Buddhism, and in modern terms is one of the major goals of Jungian psychology.

The extremes are one-sided spiritual and psychological attitudes which can only lead to total disintegration of the human spirit. They point to the need for the union of the two opposites in a new and higher integrity.

The Middle Pillar thus becomes symbolic of the 'way of return', the path of redemption, as it were. A vast system both of esoteric theory and magical practice has been erected on these structures.

The Four Worlds

Another way of looking at the Tree is by way of the Four Worlds. These levels are known as *Atziluth*, or the Archetypal World; *Briah*, the Creative World; *Yetzirah*, the Formative World, and *Assiah*, the World of Action, the Material World. These in turn are attributed to the four letters of the divine name, often referred to as the Tetragrammaton, which simply means the four-lettered name of YHVH. Now this refers not simply to the Jehovah of the Old Testament, who appears to have been a provincial, racial and testy old tutelary deity, but to the basic creative force in action of the *Ain Soph*, the Infinite. The old name is retained but is given an entirely new and broad interpretation.

Y is *Yod*, attributed to the element of fire, and is called the Father; it is the archetype of all things, and the area, as it were, of God and His divine names. H, *Heh*, the first H of Tetragrammaton, is the Mother, referred to the element of water, the creative world where the archangelic forces hold sway and function, carrying out the creative impulses received from on high. V is *Vau*, the Son, referred to the element of air, and to the Formative World, where the angelic forces fashion and form the prototypes of all things on the imaginative basis previously laid down. The final H, *Heh*, is referred to the Daughter, the element of earth, where all the intrinsic factors of the higher creative forces become embodied.

All is God and His creative energy, from the highest to the lowest – for there is nothing that is not God. It is only the limitations of our sensory structure that prevent us from perceiving that we live and move and have our being in the Godhead, here and now.

Westcott affirms that 'Man is still the copy of God on earth; his form is related to the Tetragrammaton of Jehova, YHVH, for in a diagram *Yod* is as the head, *Heh* the arms, *Vau* the body, and the final H, *Heh*,the lower limbs.'

The Pentagrammaton

One of the letters of the Hebrew alphabet is *Shin*. In the *Book of Formation* it is given the attribution of fire, and, by another mathematical process, it becomes the symbol of the Holy Spirit. Tradition sponsors the insertion of this letter into the middle of the four-lettered Name, splitting it asunder, thus forming YHshVH, the Pentagrammaton or five-lettered Name. This combination of letters represents the illumination of the elemental or natural man by the descent and impact of the Holy Spirit. As thus formed, the name represents the God-man, symbolized in Christianity by Christ descending on the man Jesus. Jesus, by this symbolism, represents the natural man who, by devotion and meditation and the theurgic process, opened his human nature to the brilliant descent of the Light.

It is this enlightenment that all men are destined to enjoy at some far-distant time in human evolution. It is this that separates man *qua* man from the God-man, the goal of all mysticism. All mystical techniques, including those of the Qabalah, represent a method of hastening the slow tedious process of human evolution so that the states of consciousness that we are told will ultimately occur routinely in mankind may dawn today.

The ten digits or files of The Tree of Life are the manifold expression of deity conceived of as the creative power of the Primal Light. This is labelled as *Ain Soph* – the Infinite, serving as the absolute, unknown and unknowable divine ground of Being. It is from this Nothingness that creation takes place, creation in and from Its essence, descending and ascending in various degrees of clarity or obscurity (to us only), resulting in the appearance of several emanations that are labelled *Sephiroth*.

Incidentally, this word *Sephiroth* is a feminine plural form of the word *Sephirah*. In *The Book of Formation* the word *Sephiroth* is variously translated as numbers, letters and sounds. Creation is conceived to be a divine magical act symbolized by the employment of the letters of the Hebrew alphabet. These letters are not merely symbols of magical forces; they *are* the creative forces of the universe. This assumed fact underlies all magical ritual and theurgic process. As one of the Golden Dawn rituals puts it: 'By names and images are all powers awakened and re-awakened.' Ritual action not only represents symbolically the divine life; it evokes the interior spiritual force manifested in concrete symbols.

I must emphasize here the fact that this is only an elementary and suggestive treatise. There is no attempt made to follow an orderly pattern of exposition. It is essentially a kind of free association that I am pursuing. When the student can follow this simple rambling exposition without too much difficulty, then he can turn with confidence to some of the more systematic and complex delineations of the system.

Kether

The firist *Sephirah* is known as *Kether*, the Crown, and represents a concentration of light-energy within the infinity of *Ain Soph*. The Qabalistic theory has it that from the Infinite Light, the creative impulse proceeded in a flash of radiant light (*Zohar*). This released the creative powers of the Infinite, resulting in a point or focus of multi-faceted potentiality and development. In addition to the Crown, it is also known as the Smooth Point, Macroprosopus or the Great Face and a host of other symbolic images and names, and is the first or opening *Sephirah* on the Tree.

In other mythologies it is represented by Amoun 'The Concealed One' and the Opener of the Day', as well as by Ptah the divine potter who forms all things on his revolving wheel. One of the several attributions of *Kether* is *Raysheeth ha-gilgoleem*, the first wheelings or whirlings – as though to imply the earliest spiral nebula movements. All beginnings, all seeds, of all things represented by One, find their place in this part of the filing cabinet. One of the really great, though less well-known, American occult teachers defines it as 'The Power to be Conscious', a very eloquent phrase.

Another of its many associations is Metatron, the Angel of the Presence who, avers the ancient mythology, was changed into a fiery flame. We know from the Bible that God is a burning fire. Yet another attribution is the choir of angels known as the *Chayoth ha-Qadesh*, translated as the Holy Living Creatures. These are the four Kerubuc Beings seen by Ezekiel in his vision. The opening of the Book of Ezekiel is worth re-reading at this juncture.

This prophet's vision of the Lord riding upon the fiery chariot of the Holy Living Creatures, accompanied by supernal visions and voices, movements and upheavals on earth – all of this well outside the range of the spiritual experiences of most other Biblical personalities – was for the Qabalist a real opening into higher realms. It represented an unveiling of the innermost and impenetrable secrets locked up in the newly-revealed interrelation of man and God. It was ever interpreted as a sort of divine self-unveiling, an ineffable mystical experience of the highest magnitude. The Qabalists considered that the door to the beyond was flung wide open so that the properly prepared individual, at the direct invitation of God, could mount as though on a flaming Pegasus and chariot to the secret spiritual life that he has laboured for so long to reach.

The chariot (the *Merkabah*) was thus a 'mystic way' leading to the veritable heights of the Tree of Life, to the Crown of all. It was considered a vehicle by means of which the Qabalist was carried directly to a face-to-face encounter with his highest divinity. It was the aim of the would-be mystic, therefore, to be a '*Merkabah*-rider' so that he might be enabled while still incarnate as a human being to ascend to his spiritual El Dorado. Enlightenment is thus the meaning of all the 'chariot' symbolisms.

Chokmah

Chokmah, or Wisdom, is the name of the second emanation or manifestation. It is alluded to above all other representations of the primal duality as fatherhood, maleness, wisdom, the positive pole – all these associations are represented here. There are archangels and angels attributed to each one of these *Sephiroth*, representing the emergence of different forms or types of the divine creative power and intent.

The divine name used in the Old Testament is said to be *Yah*. The archangel is Ratziel, the Mystery of God, while its astrological attribution refers to the wheel of the zodiac itself, as though to indicate its supraterrestrial sphere of influence.

In the prologue of the *Zohar*, the Book of Splendour, is a beautiful myth expatiating on the biblical verse 'In the beginning God created ...'. By way of preamble, it is necessary to indicate that the Hebrew words for this are '*be-Raysheeth bara Elohim* ...'. A literal translation is as follows:

B' means 'In'

Raysheeth – 'the beginning'

Bara – 'created'

Elohim – translated as God. (But the word *El* is God. *Eloh* would be a feminine God, the suffix *oh* determining the feminine gender. The other suffix *im* is a masculine form of plurality. In the word *Sephiroth*, for example, the suffix *oth* represents the feminine form of plurality.)

The first letter of the Bible therefore is B, *Beth*, as it is also of the second word *bara*, to create.

The Zoharic myth I refer to deals with the Hebrew letters as beings or personifications of the creative forces which one by one parade before God asking for the privilege of being the first to describe the process of creation: 'When the Holy One, blessed be He, was about to make the world, all the letters of the alphabet were still embryonic ... When He came to create the world, all the letters advanced themselves before Him in reversed order.'

One by one, they describe why they and they alone should be so chosen, and one by one, arguments are tendered to deny them this privilege. Finally the letter B(in Hebrew *Beth*) entered the scene, and said:

'"O Lord of the world, may it please Thee to put me first in the creation of the world, since I represent the benedictions (*berakhoth*) offered to Thee on high and below." The Holy One, blessed be He, said to her: "Assuredly, with thee I will create the world, and thou shalt form the beginning in the creation of the world."'

The entire emphasis on this play on words and letters is really to elicit the concept, so necessary for man, of the benevolence and benediction of the Creative Power. It would have been very difficult for early man to have lived without this belief.

And thus it came to be that the letter *Beth* opens up the biblical account of creation. Now, using the comparative method made possible by our filing cabinet, we find that to B, the number 2, in the *Sepher Yetzirah*, the planet Mercury is attributed, and so its god is Hermes who is a lower form of the Egyptian Thoth, the god of 'wisdom and utterance, the god that cometh forth from the veil.' Thoth is said to have pronounced the magical words that formed the whole gamut of created things. In the particular exordium of the Golden Dawn, there is the following significant passage:

At the ending of the Night; at the limits of the Light, Thoth stood
before the Unborn Ones of Time!
Then was formulated the Universe;
Then came forth the Gods thereof:
The Aeons of the Bornless Beyond:
Then was the Voice vibrated:
Then was the Name declared.
At the Threshold of the Entrance, between the Universe and the
Infinite,
In the Sign of the Enterer, stood Thoth as before him were the
Aeons proclaimed.
In Breath did he vibrate them; in Symbols did he record them.
For betwixt The Light and the Darkness did he stand.

This entire passage from the Golden Dawn teaching is worthy of
prolonged meditation. It should be related in meditation to the
following idea from Dion Fortune's book on the Qabalah:

In order to contact *Chokmah* we must experience the rush of the
dynamic cosmic energy in its pure form; an energy so tremendous
that mortal man is fused into disruption by it. It is recorded that
when Semele, mother of Dionysos, saw Zeus her divine lover in his
god-form as the Thunderer, she was blasted and burnt, and gave
birth to her divine son prematurely. The spiritual experience
assigned to *Kether* is the Vision of God face to face; and God
(Jehovah) said to Moses, 'Thou canst not look upon my face and
live.'
But although the sight of the Divine Father blasts mortals as
with fire, the Divine Son comes familiarly among them and can be
invoked by the appropriate rites – Bacchanalia in the case of the Son
of Zeus, and the Eucharist in the case of the Son of Jehovah. Thus
we see that there is a lower form of manifestation, which 'shews us
the Father', but that this rite owes its validity solely to the fact that
it derives its Illuminating Intelligence, its Inner Robe of Glory, from
the Father, *Chokmah*.

Binah

Binah, Understanding, is the third *Sephirah*, and is feminine and
negative in polarity. To *Binah* is attributed amongst other things the
Shekinah, a symbol of the Holy Spirit. This is a fascinating set of
concepts since it emerged in Judaic thought, which in its monotheism
is male-oriented without a diluting trace of any feminine influence. The
one exception possibly is in the constant devotional reference to the
Sabbath as a Bride – and on this concept a vast mystical

superstructure has been erected. It connects the Sabbath with the *Shekinah*, and while apparently using biblical texts as authority, some Qabalistic books force the emergence of a symbolism or a mythos which is in every way feminine and thus unalterably opposed to the historical development of non-mystical Judaism. It is reminiscent of Jung's idea of enantiodromia, that any psychological trend sooner or later must evoke or pass into its opposite – the Taoist idea that each element of *Yang* or *Yin* contains the seed or root of its own opposite. 'At the height of the *Yang* (the male) the *Yin* (female) is born.'

In orthodox Judaic literature, the *Shekinah* – a word meaning literally the indwelling presence of God – is taken to mean simply God himself in His omnipresent activity in the world, and of course in Israel. His presence, what the Bible calls His 'face', is in Rabbinical usage His indwelling presence in the world. Nowhere in the conventional orthodox literature is a distinction made between God Himself and His *Shekinah*. The *Shekinah* is not there a special hypostasis distinguished from God as a whole. God is transcendent; His *Shekinah* is immanent.

So far as concerns the Qabalah, however, the *Shekinah* is conceived as an aspect of God, a quasi-independent feminine element within Him. She is also conceived as the dwelling place of the human soul, an entirely new conception. The idea that man's highest self had its origin in the feminine precinct within God Himself is an outstanding and far-reaching contribution of the Qabalah to mystical thought. It bears many similarities to Eastern philosophy, especially to the Vedanta.

It at once differentiates the Qabalah from the hitherto masculine sterility of orthodox Judaic belief, so top-heavy without a feminine component, and permits a well-defined comparison, within the format of The Tree of Life, with such feminine potencies in other esoteric systems such as the Holy Ghost, Kwan Yin, Shakti, Mother Durga, Aditi the Light-mother, and Mary the mother of Jesus. They may not be wholly identical, but there remain nonetheless enormous similarities which render the possibility of concretizing a true science of comparative mystical religion.

All of this aids in our understanding of *Binah* as the great Mother, the wide open sea which has given birth to us all, the planet Saturn, sombre and grave, and old Chronos, the father of Time. Crowley has likened her to our Lady Babalon, the mother of all whoredoms – and while the language is at first startling to a degree, it accords entirely with the Eastern concept of Kali, the giver of life and death, the lover of every man, capable of infinite conceptions. Ramakrishna's devotion to Kali, to the divine Mother, is an outstanding example of this.

These three *Sephiroth* are often spoken of as the Supernals – far removed from and transcending the operations and functions of the other areas of The Tree of Life. Seen as a unity, these three are referred to simply as *Aimah Elohim*, the Mother of the Gods, to whom are given the three Vedantic characteristics of *Sat-Chit-Ananda* – Being, Wisdom and Ecstasy. Played against these are their Buddhist opposites of *Anatta, Anicca*, and *Dukkham* – Unsubstantiality, Impermanence and Sorrow. The opposites are, paradoxically, identical in this transcendent area of the Tree.

Separating the divine transcendence from the more familiar and more readily conceivable aspects of the Tree, there is said to stretch a vast gulf, an abyss between noumenon and phenomenon, which is wholly unbridgeable by man. So long as he remains man, bound up in his private world of reason and practical events, the Supernals are abstract unreachable concepts. Only by riding the *mercabah* or the mystical experience, resulting in the destruction of *ahamkara*, the ego-making faculty, can the abyss be traversed. The tradition here is so vast, so complex, and so abstract that we have to be content at this moment with just this reference, and no more.

The planetary attribution is Saturn, stability and form, form which binds energy, as *purusha* is embodied in *prakriti* according to the Sankhya system of Kapila. Its archangel is merely the Hebrew name for Saturn, *Shabbathai*, with the 'el' appended as a suffix – at least so it is according to the *Sigillum Dei Aemeth* of the Dee-Kelly system, making Shabbathiel, or Tzaphkiel in the more traditional system. The divine name is *YHVH Elohim*, a compound of Tetragrammaton plus the masculine plural of a female god.

The *Sephirah* is ambivalent, or rather, as a true symbol, bipolar. In the lovely Crowleyan symbolism, *Binah* is the City of the Pyramids under the Night of Pan, where the adept who has crossed the abyss as a successful *mercabah*-rider, and so annihilated the ego, becomes a Babe of the Abyss nursed by our Lady Babalon.

As a final comment relative to *Binah*, there is a short paragraph by Dion Fortune which is pertinent hereto:

The expansive force given off by petrol is pure energy, but it will not drive a car. The constrictive organization of *Binah* is potentially capable of driving a car, but it cannot do so unless set in motion by the expansion of the stored-up energy of petrol-vapour. *Binah* is all-potential, but inert. *Chokmah* is pure energy, limitless and tireless, but incapable of doing anything except radiate off into space if left to its own devices. But when *Chokmah* acts upon *Binah*, its energy is gathered up and set to work. When *Binah* receives the impulse of *Chokmah*, all her latent capacities are energized. Briefly, *Chokmah* supplies the energy, and *Binah* supplies the machine.

Chesed

Chesed is the next *Sephirah*. The Hebrew word means 'mercy'. All significances attached to the number 4 find their place in this filing jacket.

Jupiter is the astrological attribution, from which we obtain ideas of the authority, form, law, abundance, generosity, and order in the Eastern sense of *dharma* – the rightness of things, the proper way. Here too is to be found the Egyptian *Maat*, who wields the feather of Truth.

Its magical symbol or image is that of a crowned and powerful king enthroned on a dais, clothed with the fulsome purples and royal blues associated with his regal status. Around him are the cognate symbols of Jupiterian authority, the orb and the crook. On some of the Egyptian godforms, the crook is pointed to the left shoulder to which *Chesed* is attributed, whilst the flail or the scourge points to the right shoulder, to *Geburah*. The crook or crozier is the shepherd tool of mercy, the pastoral staff of giving aid on the spiritual level.

In this same connection, Zeus is an attribute – the god whose authority and power and energy is so vast that he commands the lightning and the storms, and hurls the thunderbolts.

Thus *Chesed* is authority and divine leadership, which produces order out of chaos, permitting freedom and liberty within certain well-defined limits. 'Liberty', wrote Dion Fortune with great sagacity, 'might be defined as the right to choose one's master, for a ruler one must have in all organized corporate life, else there is chaos. It is effectual and inspiring leadership that is the crying need of the world at the present time, and country after country is seeking and finding the ruler who approximates most closely to its national ideal, and is falling in as one man behind him. It is the benign, organizing, ordering Jupiter influence that is the only medicine for the world's sickness; as this comes to bear, the nations will recover their emotional poise and physical health.'

The geometrical form proper to this sphere is the square – reminiscent of the Masonic moral idea of being on the level, on the square; this too is *dharma*. Its Jungian archetypal symbol would probably be the 'wise old man'. Its element is water, reflected downwards from *Binah*. Each *Sephirah*, it must be noted, is a fascinating combination of balance of male and female, positive and negative symbols, in equilibrium.

Other titles for *Chesed* are *Gedulah*, greatness or majesty, and *Rachamon*, Mercy. The divine name is *El*, meaning simply God – masculine in nature and grammar. Its archangelic force is called Tzadkiel, the righteousness of God. Its angels are the *Chashmalim*, the Brilliant Ones.

It is the ancient occult view that man is a microcosm of the macrocosm, a replica in miniature of the great world in which he lives, and of which he is a part. Whatever set of forces operate in the vast expanses of the universe about him, these are also represented within man himself. Thus the Tree is not only a symbolic map of the universe; its *Sephiroth* are symbolic representatives of the psychic structure of man as well.

In fact, relative to this, there is a pertinent quotation from the *Zohar*:

> What, then, is man? Does he consist solely of skin, flesh, bones and sinews? Nay, the essence of man is his soul; the skin, flesh, bones and sinews are but an outward covering, the mere garments, but they are not the man. When man departs (from this world) he divests himself of all these garments. The skin with which he covers himself, and all these bones and sinews, all have a symbolism in the mystery of the Supernal Wisdom, corresponding to that which is above ...
>
> The bones and the sinews symbolize the Chariots and the celestial Hosts, which are inward. All these are garments upon that which is inward; which also is the mystery of the Supernal Man, who is the innermost. The same is found here below. Man is something inward, and his garments correspond to that which is above ... Esoterically, the man below corresponds entirely to the Man above.

Geburah

Geburah, Severity, is the fifth *Sephirah*. It counterbalances *Chesed* on the Tree, and in terms of Qabalistic theory is the opposite. Whereas the fourth *Sephirah* represents mercy and kindness and form-building through love and attraction, *Geburah* represents power and energy and, inversely, destruction and tearing down. Both are cosmic processes as well as endopsychic events, neither to be denied or underestimated. If there were only building-up and construction, the universe would soon become a rather cluttered place – the vision of our already over-crowded cities on a cosmic scale. The power involved here ensures that outmoded forms of life and ways of communication, whatever they may be, are broken down and the material re-employed in other and more suitable ways.

It is nicely expressed in Dion Fortune's book in these well-chosen words:

> Dynamic energy is as necessary to the welfare of society as meekness, charity, and patience. We must never forget that the

eliminatory diet, which will restore health in disease, will produce disease in health. We must never exalt the qualities which are necessary to compensate an overplus of force into ends in themselves and the means of salvation. Too much charity is the handiwork of a fool; too much patience is the hall-mark of a coward. What we need is a just and wise balance which makes for health, happiness, and sanity all round, and the frank realization that sacrifices are necessary to obtain it. You cannot eat your cake and have it in the spiritual sphere any better than anywhere else.

The divine name is appropriately *Elohim Gibor*, a Powerful God, or the Gods (male and female) of Might. Its planet is Mars, the god of War, expressing the character of Ra Hoor Khuit in *The Book of the Law*: 'Now let it be first understood that I am a god of War and of Vengeance. I shall deal hardly with them ... Worship me with fire & blood; worship me with swords & with spears. Let the woman be girt with a sword before me: let blood flow to my name.'

In the book of Exodus, there is a paean of martial joy to Jehovah after the crossing of the Red Sea which had opened up for the children of Israel to pass through, and then closed over the Egyptians with their chariots, destroying them wholly. There He is called *Eesh milchomah*, a Man of War. 'Jehovah is a mighty warrior; Jehovah is His Name!' I can still vividly remember from early boyhood attending the synagogue when this particular portion of the *Torah* was being sung. The entire melody and style of ritual chanting changed triumphantly as the cantor entoned: 'I will sing unto Jehovah, for he hath triumphed gloriously! ... Thy right hand, O Jehovah, is become glorious in power; thy right hand O Lord hath dashed the enemy to pieces! ... Who is like unto Thee among the Gods, O Jehovah!' (The Hebrew initials of this last sentence were used centuries later to form the neologism 'Macabee'.) No one listening could fail to have the blood freeze in his veins, and the hackles arise on the back of his neck.

Geburah, in a word, is the energy aspect of creativity. All the symbols, from any source, mythological or otherwise, relate exclusively to this notion. Since it is the fifth file in our filing system, all five pointed figures, symbols, ideas, and so forth, are referred here.

Aleister Crowley once wrote a charming little pornographic story called *The Daughter of the Horseleech* which in itself is of no consequence to us here, save for the one redeeming feature of a beautiful description of the entire spiritual hierarchy of *Geburah*, from the divine Name down to the lowliest spirit. It is so well done that it is worth-while quoting the several paragraphs as descriptive of the hierarchical elements:

The crown of *Elohim Gibor* was Space itself; the two halves of his brain were the Yea and Nay of the Universe; his breath was the breath of very Life; his being was the Mahalingam of the First, beyond Life and Death the generator from Nothingness. His armour was the Primal Water of Chaos. The infinite moonlike curve of his body; the flashing swiftness of his Word, that was the Word that formulated that which was beyond Chaos and Cosmos; the might of him, greater than that of the Elephant and of the Lion and of the Tortoise and of the Bull fabled in Indian legend as the supports of the four letters of the Name; the glory of him, that was even as that of the Sun which is before all and beyond all Suns, of which the stars are little sparks struck off as he battled in the Infinite against the Infinite ...

Behold the mighty one, behold *Kamael* the strong! His crownless head was like a whirling wheel of amethyst, and all the forces of the earth and heaven revolved therein. His body was the Mighty Sea itself, and it bore the scars of crucifixion that had made it two score times stronger than it was before. He too bore the wings and weapons of Space and Justice; and in himself he was that great Amen that is the beginning and end of all.

Behind him were the *Seraphim*, the fiery Serpents. On their heads the triple tongues of fire; their glory like unto the Sun, their scales like burning plates of steel; they danced like virgins before their lord, and upon the storm and roar of the sea did they ride in their glory ...

All glorious was the moon-like crown of the great Intelligence *Graphiel*. His face was like the Sun as it appears beyond the veil of this earthly firmament. His warrior body was like a tower of steel, virginal strong.

Scarlet were his kingly robes, and his limbs were swathed in young leaves of lotus; for those limbs were stronger than any armour ever forged in heaven or hell. Winged was he with the wings of gold that are the Wind itself; his sword of green fire flamed in his right hand, and in his left he held the blue feather of Justice, unstirred by the wing of his flight, or the upheaval of the universe.

Bartzabel ... Of flaming, radiant, far-darting gold was his crown; flashing hither and thither more swiftly than the lightning were its rays. His head was like the Sun in its strength, even at high noon. His cloak was of pure amethyst, flowing behind him like a mighty river; his armour was of living gold, burnished with lightning even to the greaves and the armed feet of him; he radiated an intolerable splendour of gold and he bore the Sword and balance of Justice. Mighty and golden were his wide-flashing wings!

Tiphareth

Tiphareth (pronounced T'phay-reth) means Beauty, harmony and infers Equilibrium and balance. On The Tree of Life it is the central *Sephirah*, and in many ways is one of the most important sections of our filing cabinet. It is equidistant, as it were, to *Kether* as it is from *Malkuth*, and it has connecting links with practically every other part of the Tree.

The magical images which give meaning to the file are manifold. They include the resurrection gods of every age and clime from Osiris to Christ, the solar discs from Ra to Apollo, gods of spiritual inebriation such as Bacchus and Dionysos, and the newly born spiritual child from Krishna to baby Jesus. Meditation on all of these images will reveal the essential nature of the *Sephirah*.

As usual, Dion Fortune expresses herself extremely well in this connection:

> The ancients ... differentiated between the mantic methods which induced the chthonic, or underworld contacts, and the divine inebriation of the Mysteries. The Maenads rushing in the train of Dionysos were of an entirely different order of initiation to the pythonesses; the pythonesses were psychics and mediums, but the Maenads, the initiates of the Dionysiac Mysteries, enjoyed exaltation of consciousness and a quickening of life that enabled them to perform amazing prodigies of strength.
>
> All the dynamic religions have this Dionysiac aspect; even in the Christian religion many saints have left record of the Crucified Christ of their devotion coming to them at last as the Divine Bridegroom; and when they speak of this divine inebriation that comes to them, their language uses the metaphors of human love as its appropriate expression – 'How lovely art thou, my sister, my spouse'; 'Faint from the kisses of the lips of God ...' These things tell a great deal to those who have understanding.

Its more immediate astrological symbol is the sun with its almost infinite number of attributions and significances, which should be studied and meditated upon to get the full impact of the *Sephirah*.

Its divine name is *YHVH Eloah ve-Daath*, rather difficult or meaningless to translate literally, but may be rendered as YHVH, Lord God of Knowledge. The archangel is Raphael, the healing of God, which might remind us of Exodus, 15:26: 'For I am the Lord that healeth thee.' *Malachim* is a Hebrew word meaning angels; if the second 'a' is omitted, it may be translated as 'kings'.

Perhaps one of the best ways of elucidating the full meaning of this

Sephirah is to quote one of the Golden Dawn ritual speeches from a document known as Z-1:

> For Osiris on-Nophris who is found perfect before the Gods, hath said:
>> These are the Elements of my Body.
>> Perfected through suffering, glorified through trial.
> For the scent of the dying rose is as the repressed sigh of my suffering:
>> And the flame-red fire as the energy of mine undaunted will;
>> And the cup of Wine is the pouring out of the blood of my Heart.
>> Sacrificed unto regeneration, unto the newer Life.
>> And the bread and salt are as the foundations of my body
>> Which I destroy in order that they may be renewed.
> For I am Osiris triumphant, even Osiris on-Nophiris the Justified.
>> I am He who is clothed with the body of flesh,
>> Yet in whom is the Spirit of the great Gods.
>> I am the Lord of Life, triumphant over death.
>> He who partaketh with me shall arise with me;
> I am the manifestor in matter of Those whose abode is the Invisible.
>> I am purified: I stand upon the universe.
>> I am its reconciler with the eternal Gods.
>> I am the Perfector of Matter.
>> And without me, the Universe is not.

Netzach

Netzach, Victory, is the seventh section of our filing cabinet. By using the English translation, we can consider *Nike*, with a firm stride forward, with wings apart and ablaze with fire and fury, as the symbolic image for our meanings.

The divine name *YHVH Tzabaoth*, Lord God of Hosts, is equally confirmatory of this theme. We are not dealing with creative imagination here, or with any mental faculty in the ordinary sense of the term, but with the fire of emotion and feeling, which basically are the forces that evoke creativity. These are not merely constituents of the human psyche; they are integral components of the universe itself. The experience of ecstasy, joy, delight and fervour – this is Victory.

Its fire is reflected from *Geburah*, making a well-defined relationship between the astrological polarities of Mars and Venus.

The pantheons filed here are those relating to the astrological attribution of Venus itself. Aphrodite, Astarte, Hathor, and so forth.

They represent love, fulfilment, pleasure, the arts in all their forms, and beauty.

Just as in a horoscope, the seventh house represents marriage, but the fifth house represents pleasure, creativity, and sex, so *Netzach* may include love, pleasure and sexuality (or polarity), but it is *Yesod* which refers to productivity and fertility. There is no necessary relationship between one and the other; each may co-exist by itself.

Netzach refers to the emotions and feelings which may bring about a union of the two poles, but it is *Yesod* and the moon and its inner psychic tides that permit this coupling to result in offspring.

Netzach may be said to refer to the desire-nature, to what the East calls *Kama*, desire, wish, need, lust.

The approach to God, as a technical mystical way of life, relating to this sphere is *bhakta*, devotion and love. Crowley's *Liber Astarte vel Berylli* is certainly worth reading in this connection, and the following is one small quotation from this devotional text to elicit the full flavour of *bhakta* and *Netzach*.

Let the devotee consider well that although Christ and Osiris be one, yet the former is to be worshipped with Christian, and the latter with Egyptian, rites. And this, although the rites themselves are ceremonially equivalent. There should, however, be *one* symbol declaring the transcending of such limitations; and with regard to the Deity also, there should be some *one* affirmation of his identity both with all other similar gods of other nations, and with the Supreme of whom all are but partial reflections.

Concerning the chief place of devotion: This is the Heart of the Devotee, and should be symbolically represented by that room or spot which he loves best. And the dearest spot therein shall be the shrine of his temple. It is most convenient if this shrine and altar should be sequestered in woods, or in a private grove, or garden. But let it be protected from the profane.

Concerning the Image of the Deity: Let there be an image of the Deity; first because in meditation there is mindfulness induced thereby; and second because a certain power enters and inhabits it by virtue of the ceremonies; or so it is said, and we deny it not. Let this image be the most beautiful and perfect which the devotee is able to procure; or if he be able to paint or to carve the same, it is all the better. As for Deities with whose nature no Image is compatible, let them be worshipped in an empty shrine ...

Concerning the Ceremonies: Let the Philosophus prepare a powerful Invocation of the particular Deity according to his Ingenium. But let it consist of these several parts:

First, an Imprecation, as of a slave unto his Lord.

Second, an Oath, as of a vassal to his Liege.
Third, a Memorial, as of a child to his Parent.
Fourth, an Orison, as of a Priest unto his God.
Fifth, a Colloquy, as of a Brother with his Brother.
Sixth, a Conjuration, as to a Friend with his Friend.
Seventh, a Madrigal, as of a Lover to his Mistress.

And mark well that the first should be of awe, the second of fealty, the third of dependence, the fourth of adoration, the fifth of confidence, the sixth of comradeship, the seventh of passion.

This is the essential spirit of *Netzach*.

Hod

Hod is Glory, and in this eighth file we have all the mercurial gods, stressing the notion that here we have the mental and intellectual. It has a watery attribution, reflected from *Chesed*, so that there is a well-defined connection between Jupiter, the so-called higher mind, and Mercury, lower or the concrete forms of mental activity. Some of the modern writers consider *Hod* as a 'form' *Sephirah* as opposed to the 'force' concept of *Netzach*. It is the area of mental images on the inner plane and intellectual effort.

If we take the ancient phrase 'God geometrizes' and then add 'God philosophizes' we have something implied of the nature of *Hod*. Its attribution to Mercury is further indicative of its essential nature, for like the metal mercury, this phase of mental activity in man is eternally in a flux, never still for a moment. The description of the Roman or Greek Mercury is eloquent in describing the area of mental activity implied by *Hod*. A mythological dictionary asserts that Hermes was the god of commerce, wealth and good fortune as well as the messenger or herald of the gods. He seems also to have been the patron deity of tricksters, travellers, glib talkers and thieves. In early Greek history, he was also known as a fertility god, and interestingly enough, crude phallic images of him called *hermae* were set up at crossroads and in front of houses. Like the Egyptian Anubis, the dog-headed watcher of the temples, he was considered to be a psychopomp, the conductor of departed souls through the after-death states.

The magical image is said to be a hermaphrodite. The name also used was Hermanubis, a combination of Hermes of the Greeks and Anubis of the Egyptians. The hermaphrodite or bi-sexual implies that Mercury or *Hod* is the area of thought-forms and is largely neutral and sexless; or let us say that its polarity is larval, depending upon the use to which these forms can be put by the ensouling emotional factors.

The divine name is *Elohim Tzabaoth*, the God of Hosts – the *Elohim*, let us recall from an earlier page, being in Hebrew the male plural termination of the singular female 'god'. This is opposed to *YHVH Tzabaoth* of *Netzach*, which is Jehovah of Hosts or Armies. The archangel is said to be Michael, who is like God, and then we have to recall that of all the planets Mercury is that which is nearest the sun and reflects the light of the sun more clearly than any other planet or satellite.

Just as the practical approach of *Netzach* is *bhakta*, so the *Hod* approach is *gnana*, philosophy. It is worthy of note that in Crowley's reformulation of the Golden Dawn, the specific tasks he prescribed for the grade attributed to *Hod* were the mastery of philosophy and above all of the Qabalah itself. Emphasis was directed for example to its mathematical parts so that any number might be fully investigated and understood in terms of its intrinsic formula.

Appropriately, there is in Dion Fortune's book this statement:

If we have no magical capacity, which is the work of the intellectual imagination, the Sphere of *Hod* will be a closed book to us. We can only operate in a Sphere after we have received the initiation of that Sphere, which, in the language of the Mysteries, confers its powers. In the technical working of the Mysteries these initiations are conferred on the physical plane by means of ceremonial, which may be effectual, or may not. The gist of the matter lies in the fact that one cannot waken into activity that which is not already latent. Life is the real initiator; the experiences of life stimulate into function the capacities of our temperaments in such degree as we possess them. The ceremony of initiation, and the teachings that should be given in the various grades, are simply designed to make conscious what was previously subconscious, and to bring under the control of the will, directed by the higher intelligence, those developed reaction-capacities which have hitherto only responded blindly to their appropriate stimuli.

Yesod

Yesod, the Foundation, is the area of the lunar gods and those who preside over fertility, animal or vegetative. It is also the area of sex, so that, without effort, this part of the filing cabinet can become extensive. Its magical image is that of a very strong naked man, capable of bearing large and heavy burdens – classically, Atlas holding the world on his shoulders. The Egyptian one is not dissimilar – Shu, the god of the air, who separates the sky-goddess Nuit from Geb, the god of the earth. Just to round out the symbolism, there is, paradoxically, the notion of the fundamental three phases of the moon, their deity attributions, and their functions in women. There is Artemis, or Selene, the young virginal goddess, huntress, chaste, innocent and pure – the moon in the opening days of her cycle. This is followed by the full moon, representing the fecund and fertile Mother, in full production as it were, fulfilling herself joyously in her basic generative function, symbolized by Aphrodite. This is the fertile and, because fulfilled, loved and loving woman in her prime. Then follows the moon in her decline, the waning moon, Hecate, the post-menopausal woman who has found no substitute fulfilment now that her child-bearing days are gone, she resents the loss of love and loving now that her sexual attractiveness has vanished, becoming embittered, sullen, skinny, and hag-like. This old crone who has no family, feared and hated because of her sharp masculinized tongue, was in old times suspected of witchcraft, and became altogether isolated.

Robert Graves expresses this extraordinarily well in the Introduction to his book *The Greek Myths*:

> Since the sun's annual course similarly recalled the rise and decline of her physical powers – spring a maiden, a summer a nymph, winter a crone – the goddess became identified with seasonal changes in animal and plant life; and thus with Mother Earth who, at the beginning of the vegetative year, produces only leaves and buds, then flowers and fruits, and at last ceases to bear. She could later be conceived as yet another triad; the maiden of the upper air, the nymph of the earth or the sea, the crone of the underworld – typified by Selene, Aphrodite, and Hecate. These mystical analogues fostered the sacredness of the number three, and the Moon-goddess became enlarged to nine when each of the three persons – maiden, nymph, and crone – appeared in triad to demonstrate her divinity. Her devotees never quite forget that there were not three goddesses, but one goddess.

We are dealing with the generative power of nature which coordinates, integrates and stimulates the chemistry of our bodies, and the larger body of the earth we live on, and the chemistry of the solar and stellar systems in which we live. It is not a product of physical life, though it may seem to be so. It is, however, the power behind the scenes, as it were, activating the molecules, cells and tissues. Thus, it led to the concept of a hidden area behind or within nature which is the electro-magnetic model or energy-field shaping the protoplasm within that field. So that we have the theory of the etheric or astral world which preserves the stability of the material world and provides the invisible models for all things here below that can only be changed by altering the invisible astral fields and images. Modern notions of radiant energy are held referrable here.

The divine name is *Shaddai El Chai*, Almighty Living God, the lord of generation, the indwelling divinity of the pelvis. The archangel is said to be Gabriel, the might of God who oversees the angels, who are the *Ishim*, the flames referred to in Psalms, 104:4.

Its element is air, and this The Tree of Life depicts as reflected down the middle pillar from *Kether* to *Tiphareth*, and thence to *Yesod*, the sphere of generation. About this topic, Dion Fortune wrote some years ago:

In dealing with the rhythms of Luna we are dealing with etheric, not physical, conditions. The magnetism of living creatures waxes and wanes with a definite tide. It is a thing that is not difficult to observe when one knows what to look for. It shows itself most clearly in relations between persons in whom magnetism is fairly evenly balanced. Sometimes one will be in the ascendant, and sometimes the other.

Now, it may be asked, if the Sphere of *Yesod* is etheric, why are the generative organs assigned to this sphere, for surely their function is physical, if anything is? The answer to that question is to be found in the knowledge of the subtler aspects of sex which appears to be entirely lost to the Western world ... We must liken it to an iceberg, five-sixths of whose bulk is below the surface. The actual physical reactions of sex form a very small proportion, and by no means the most vital portion of its functioning.

Malkuth

Malkuth, the Kingdom, is the tenth and final emanation in our filing system, the inferior representative of *Binah*, and in the *Zohar* she is called the Lower or Inferior Mother, *Malkah* the Queen and *Kallah* the Bride of Tetragrammaton.

Some of the symbols speak of *Malkuth* as a gate, the Gate of Death, the Gate of Tears, and even the Gate of the Daughter of the Mighty Ones. Some of these are drawn from the beautiful and sonorous titles given to the Tarot Cards. *Malkuth* is not a closed sphere; it leads always to the higher or interior *Sephiroth*; the gate is always open if we can but see it. She is also called 'The Virgin of the World', and some of the alchemical documents describe her, as the first matter of the Great Work, in some detail.

The divine Name is *Adonai ha-Aretz*, Lord of the Earth and its archangel is Sandalphon, and its choir of angels are said to be the Kerubim, the rulers of the elements. Above all other things it is the realm of the element earth, though the conventional charts of The Tree split up the sphere of *Malkuth* into areas representing the four elements themselves. This *Sephirah* on The Tree symbolizes matter, the material world itself.

As Dr Westcott wrote:

The Kabalah teaches that one must entirely relinquish the apparent knowledge of matter as an entity apart from spirit. The assertion that matter exists, and is an entity entirely different from Spirit, and that Spirit – the God of Spirits – created it, must be denied, and the notion must be torn out by the roots before progress can be made. If matter exists it is something, and must have come from something; but Spirit is not a thing, and creative Spirit, the highest Spiritual conception, could not make matter, the lowest things, out of nothing; hence it is not made, and hence there is no matter. All is Spirit and conception. *Ex nihilo nihil fit.* All that does exist can only have come from Spirit, from Divine Essence. That Being should arise from non-being is impossible. That matter should create itself is absurd; matter cannot proceed from Spirit; the two words mean that the two ideas are entirely apart; then matter cannot exist. Hence it follows that what we call matter is but an aspect, a conception, an illusion, a mode of motion, a delusion of our physical senses.

This is what Korzybski, the general semanticist, would have called the outmoded Aristotelian kind of thinking. A modern mystic, Vitvan, has attempted to conjoin general semantics or non-Aristotelian thought with the ancient wisdom, and has formulated some fascinating and highly creative concepts. Basic to his assumptions is the notion of identity – 'identification of images appearing substantive in an individual's psychic nature, with that from which stimuli (energy wave-lengths and frequencies) are received.'

Here is the great value in *conscious* abstracting, because by this process one learns to differentiate between an image-in-the psychic-nature and configurations of units of energy constituting this world. ('Forms' was Plato's name for these we call configurations.)

As an image appears on the photographic plate in a camera, so energy wave-lengths and frequencies are formulated as a picture in the mental functions of an individual's psychic nature. When this picture, due to the various neural and brain processes, *appears 'out there'*, i.e., substantive, it becomes identified with a given configuration of units of energy from which stimuli are received, then that image-appearing-substantive in the psychic nature becomes designated, labeled, etc., 'a thing', 'object', etc ...

In the totality, this formulation of qualities into mental images, constitutes what we call 'the objective world'. This identification and belief therein represents what we called 'the error'.

This intellectual error that Vitvan refers to is prevalent in many metaphysical systems including Christian Science as well as Vedanta – the delusion of matter, the notion that the world is Maya as the Orientals would say. It is also stressed in Westcott's interpretation of the non-existence of matter, due no doubt to his having been considerably influenced by association with Madame H.P. Blavatsky and the Eastern School of esotericism.

Be that as it may, the important notion to be derived from this is that *Malkuth*, the tenth *Sephirah*, is the Divine Kingdom. The world we inhabit is a divine world, and it is only due to the spiritual fog we live in, the blindness of our minds due to the limitations of our sensory systems, that we fail to perceive it as the living body of God. Only children, lovers, many artists – poets, painters and writers – and mystics have been able to see *Malkuth* as it really is, and not as a dead, empty shell. They see it, as did Thomas Traherne, who reported his vision of reality in *Centuries of Meditation:*

The corn was orient and immortal wheat, which never should be reaped, nor was ever sown. I thought it had stood from everlasting to everlasting. The dust and the stones of the street were as precious as gold; the gates were at first the end of the world. The green trees when I saw them first through one of the gates, transported and ravished me, their sweetness and unusual beauty made my heart to leap, and almost mad with ecstasy, they were such strange and wonderful things. The men! O what venerable and reverend creatures did the aged seem! Immortal Cherubim! and the young men glittering and sparkling angels, and maids, strange seraphic pieces of life and beauty. Boys and girls tumbling in the street, and playing, were moving jewels ... I know not that they were born or should die. But all things abided eternally as they were in their proper places. Eternity was manifest in the Light of the Day, and something infinite behind everything appeared.

To complete this simple discussion of the Tree of Life, I can think of nothing more fitting than Paul F. Case's 'Pattern on the Trestleboard'. It has a distinct metaphysical flavour, since there has been in the

United States a well-defined interplay between the metaphysical and occult movements. In this particular instance I think both may have profited.

THE PATTERN ON THE TRESTLEBOARD

This is the Truth about the Self.

0. All the power that ever was or will be is here now.

1. I am a centre of expression for the Primal Will-to-Good which eternally creates and sustains the universe.

2. Through me its unfailing Wisdom takes form in thought and word.

3. Filled with Understanding of its perfect law, I am guided, moment by moment, along the path of liberation.

4. From the exhaustless riches of its Limitless Substance, I draw all things needful, both spiritual and material.

5. I recognize the manifestation of the undeviating Justice in all the circumstances of my life.

6. In all things, great and small, I see the Beauty of the divine expression.

7. Living from that Will, supported by its unfailing Wisdom and Understanding, mine is the Victorious Life.

8. I look forward with confidence to the perfect realization of the Eternal Splendour of the Limitless Light.

9. In thought and deed, I rest my life, from day to day, upon the sure Foundation of Eternal Being.

10. The Kingdom of Spirit is embodied in my flesh.*

*For kind permission to quote this 'Pattern on the Trestleboard' I must acknowledge the generosity of Mrs Harriet Case, the widow of the late Paul F. Case (founder of the B.O.T.A).

FURTHER READING

Once the student has learned to feel at home intellectually with these elementary Qabalistic concepts and can function to some extent with them, he will then be ready to turn his attention to some of the more serious or more comprehensive texts.

In the order given, I strongly recommend the following for further reading:

1. *Introduction to the Kaballah*, William Wynn Westcott.
2. *The Kabbalah*, Christian D. Ginsburg.
3. *The Mystical Qabalah*, Dion Fortune.
4. *Practical Course in Qabalistic Symbolism*, Gareth Knight.
5. *Liber 777*, Aleister Crowley.
6. *Kaballah Unveiled*, Introduction by MacGregor Mathers.
7. *The Secret Doctrine in Israel*, A.E. Waite.
8. *Sepher Yetzirah*, Translated by William Wynn Westcott.
9. *On the Kaballah and its Symbolism*, G.G. Scholem.
10. *Apocalypse Unveiled*, James Pryse.
11. *The Tarot*, Paul F. Case.
12. *The Seven Rays of Q.B.L*, Frater Albertus Spagyricus, (Paracelsus Research Society, Salt Lake City, 1968).

3. MEDITATION

A Modern Approach to an Age-old Science and Art

In one of his many books, the late Paul Foster Case, perhaps the greatest of modern authorities on the significance of the traditional Tarot and Qabalah, described one of his old experiences with concentration and meditation. For at least ten long months, he said, he steadfastly practised concentration at least twice daily for about half an hour, without achieving any tangible results whatsoever. He just worked patiently, and continued to work further. Some ten months afterwards, the first results began to show. His labour paid off. He had had the patience and perseverance to keep to a disciplined schedule. Regardless of how dull, tedious and uninspiring such daily practice could be, he proved is own dedication to the Great Work.

In reality this is the story of any single person who proposes to gain some degree of mastery over the processes of his own mind. Innumerable examples could be quoted here to corroborate this dogmatic statement; but one is enough.

More rhetoric has been written on this topic than almost any other I know – with the exception of Magic. Students are misled by innumerable books about 'going into the silence', 'dwelling in the secret place of the Most High', and 'transcendental meditation', and many more grandiloquent phrases. With only a minor exception here and there, few of them emphasize the all-important fact that only discipline and constant practice are the royal factors that lead anywhere in this art. Affirmations about the nature of God and the Graces of God, and an infinite number of metaphysical variations on this theme, without daily practice of concentration, lead ultimately nowhere, regardless of the frequency of the reiterations.

Most students claiming to meditate are merely wool-gathering, which is awfully easy, indulging in vague reveries which accomplish next to nothing, save for inducing a 'good feeling' temporarily. But this is neither concentration nor meditation, and is essentially worthless.

Periodically I hear of someone, without any previous technical training, going for several days to a retreat, to spend the greater part of each waking day in prayer and meditation. For the life of me, it is difficult to imagine what goes on in their minds for the sixteen hours supposedly devoted to meditation.

No! I do not really wonder any more. After years of intimate psychological consultation with people from all walks of life and most vocations, it is my considered opinion that most of them have no talent whatsoever for concentration in any but the most superficial manner. A lawyer, accountant, engineer, physician and similar professionals have indeed developed some capacity for concentration. The years of study and intellectual preparation for their profession demanded its development. But this mental faculty operates only when functioning in a wide mental set. If their minds are forced to narrow down the broad spectrum of activity to concentrate on a single symbol, for example, at once the mental defect is demonstrable. It is widespread and an integral part of our culture.

Training the Mind

How people ever discovered the need for concentration, 'to hinder the modifications of the thinking principle', is not difficult to imagine. I suppose while performing their devotions of whatever kind – the devotions of love-making, of praying to their own particular deity, or working at their own appointed task – they must have discovered the natural ease the mind has to wander off at a tangent, and roam all over the universe.

Usually, for the untrained person, only a profound emotion will spontaneously bring about a degree of concentration. And this has to be a most intense feeling, rarely something an individual can produce to order on demand. Love, anger, jealousy and envy are capable of excluding from the mind all thoughts and feelings save that particular one.

Another factor that can produce concentration spontaneously is a very strong physical sensation – regardless of whether it be pleasure or pain. I presume that more or less everyone, at some time or other, has experienced an intense headache, toothache, or a pain somewhere in the body, that has become intense enough to thrust all other considerations to the outside of the mental periphery.

These two facts must be of some vital importance. Ultimately, they can be harnessed to the task of training the mind to concentrate at will and then to meditate.

Why Meditate?

Why should one bother to learn first to concentrate, and then to meditate? Why bother with so difficult a task? This question has to be answered in a variety of different ways, for there are as many answers as there are fundamentally different drives that motivate people.

One person may seek power; another peace and surcease from inner tensions; a third will yearn for love and heightened creativity. All motives are valid. For, in the end, all of these will be seen as facets of one major result. For meditation does result in the acquisition of spiritual power, in peace and joy, and an enhancement of the ability of the self to express itself in love and genius. So the prime motive is to discover and to realize the self.

If you happen to be a Christian, meditation is the ideal way of discovering the Christ within, of bringing the Christ-child to birth within one's soul. If you are a Hindu, then by these means one pursues the classical pathway to become aware of Atman, the Universal Self, and its essential identity with Brahman; and the meditation practice will help point the way, if you are a Buddhist, to becoming conscious of the Buddha-nature, the Transcendental Wisdom, the essence of mind that is intrinsically pure.

There are many ways by which this journey of discovery may be made. But concentration and meditation have to be considered within the category of major methods.

The Power of Meditation

Concentration is a method that has long been used successfully by some of the greatest spiritual giants that have blessed the burgeoning history of mankind.

The eternally enacted drama is that a man who is actually a nobody goes away, no one knows why or, generally, where. After a lapse of years, he returns to his home town or native country, a changed person. He is enlightened. Something strange and wonderful has happened to him. There is an air of quiet but vigorous authority about him. It is widely recognized that the mantle of inspiration cloaks him. Forthwith he begins to teach a new law, a new doctrine, a new way of approaching the divine mystery – the nature of the inner core of man. This new way promises to bring about joy and the cessation of anxiety and sorrow. It is said that the new way will ally man with the cosmic sources of power and strength and wisdom. It is unequivocally asserted that it is a way for all men, not for a special few, so that all men may attain.

And in so preaching, these hitherto unknown men stir up a hornet's nest and, attracting to themselves hordes of followers and believers, at the same time invite ridicule and severe persecution from established and entrenched authority. One has only to examine superficially the history of Moses, Buddha, Jesus and Mohammed, to name but a few of the great names that first come to mind, to recognize the universality of the dramatic theme. And at the heart of this periodical shake-up of mankind is the practice of concentration and meditation, sometimes known as interior prayer.

Once one has decided that a meditative discipline is essential, there are a few fundamentals that should be observed. I say *should* rather than *must*, because the emphasis will vary from person to person.

Posture

The Orientals lay great stress on posture as a preliminary requisite. Their textbooks describe the most complex physical manoeuvres in order to find the right kind of meditative posture, and then elaborate fantastic rationalizations as to what happens physically in order to justify them. It is worth remembering that posture of the yoga variety comes easily to the Hindus because these people have assumed these postures naturally all their lives. They have not become addicted to sitting in or on chairs of a dozen different varieties as we have as a part of our daily existence. The lotus position of one form or another is something they have done all their lives without special significance or importance being attached to it. One has only to watch children at play to realize the magnificence of their muscular flexibility and the ease with which they are able to slide in and out of these otherwise difficult positions. There is only a small percentage of Westerners, Europeans and Americans, for whom the mastery of this posture is a distinct possibility, and for whom it represents no challenge, no major difficulty.

There is really only one rule to follow concerning a meditative position. Patanjali once wrote that that posture that is easy and comfortable is right, and that is the only point that is of significance for us. If you can do it easily, or perhaps after some little practice, by all means proceed to use it daily as your own personal posture. However, should you not be one of these people (I personally am not, despite years of painful practice), reconcile yourself to sitting upright in a good upholstered chair, so that your feet are set comfortably on the floor and your spine rests easily against the back of the chairs. If necessary, stuff a small pillow against the chair opposite to the small of the back to prevent you from leaning too far back. The head and neck should be held erect.

Make a point of practising daily, sitting upright, hands folded in lap, for some several minutes, not more than ten at first, without moving a muscle or shifting position. The most important part of this instruction is the *daily* practise.

Bodily Awareness

Make a point of letting your mind roam all over your body to become aware of minor discomforts and the locus of muscular tensions. This is most important. Under no circumstances make any effort to separate your mind, your awareness, from these bodily sensations. There is a great temptation to do this, to think of something else to distract one's mind from discomfort. This tendency must be resisted at all costs. The mere fact of watching these muscular and visceral sensations, and observing them in order to separate them into ever more discrete and subtle sensations, will go far towards producing a state of physical relaxation that exceeds anything you can conceive of at this moment. And this is altogether separate from the gains of the process itself – self-realization and integrity of the whole man.

While practising, my suggestion is that the eyes be kept closed. Some schools of meditation, usually the Zen, prefer that the eyes be kept, not fully closed, but half-closed and non-focused, or with the eyes lowered. The motive for this recommendation is, among other things, usually fear that with his eyes closed, the student may go to sleep. The half-closed position may avoid this. There is some validity to this, because when the body begins to relax, whether sitting up or lying down, the average student is so unaccustomed to relaxation that the chances are he will slip involuntarily or unwittingly into a deep sleep state. Normally, I do not object to his. My attitude is, first of all, that the ensuing sleep is of very short duration. Second, as one gets used to relaxing in this or any other position, there will be less and less likelihood of sleep developing, and the alert attitude maintained.

The best stance is a condition of almost total bodily relaxation, while at the same time the mind is altogether wide-awake and vigilant. It has been described as being 'braced'. So, the eyes being closed is not by any means a liability, even if the unwanted state of sleep does occur in the opening phases or sessions of practice. Besides, with the eyes closed, innumerable external stimuli are removed that otherwise would interfere with the exploration of the inner world. Other stimuli from far different areas of the psyche are still active, of course, but these are worthy of note and actually, upon observation and examination, enlarge the horizons of the psyche.

Doubts and Fears

If you have a separate room that can be reserved solely for your meditative work, so much the better. The burning of a stick of incense, and lighing a candle, may assist in the production of a devotional mood that may conceivably dispose to working hard. But if there is no extra room available, and if incense cannot be burned nor a candle lighted, do not under any circumstances regard these facts as obstacles nor consider yourself doomed.

This latter attitude usually turns out to be a rationalization, a psychic defence mechanism, to protect oneself against the innumerable doubts about one's ability to succeed, or the fear that if one does learn to meditate, nothing will ever come of it. One is required to face oneself with as much honesty as possible.

Here, especially, is the value of a teacher. In so far as he is objective, he can help the student confront his doubts, his dishonesties, and his rationalizations. This confrontation will go far to assist in knuckling down to the hard and serious work of practice. But if there is no teacher available one must handle these probelms oneself. In any event, the room and candle and incense have but small value. The larger value is in the daily persistent exercise.

Coupled with this, the student should take advantage of some of the known facts about conditioning. At least one of the practice periods of the day should certainly be arranged to take place at the same hour, every day, without fail. In this manner, both mind and body become accustomed to settling down to the self-imposed discipline by the process of conditioning. Practising at the same hour every day sets up a favourable psychological pattern that predisposes towards success.

The Ethical Question

Authorities on the subject of meditation usually devote some consideration to the subject of ethics and morality. Complex rules of conduct and behaviour are laid down dogmatically, with the assertion that they are as inviolable as the laws of the Medes and Persians. We are told that they are important preliminaries to the work on hand.

In point of fact, however, it will be discovered that they are of no consequence whatsoever. The only point the student has to observe is that he shall do nothing to disturb his mental and emotional equilibrium. Doing so would only render concentration more difficult.

The mind is hard enough to control at best; to engage in questionable activities that have an obsessional effect on the mind, and that will preoccupy one in spite of one's best intentions, is certainly unsound policy.

Disturbing Factors

One can therefore set up certain (arbitrary) rules to facilitate the development of an attitude that will pose as few difficulties as possible. Quarrelling with one's mate is certainly inadvisable. If one must fight, then fight enthusiastically and get it over with so that the mind does not dwell on it for hours afterwards. Above all, the mental debate kind of activity has to be avoided. That is to say, while ruminating or stewing over the results of the quarrel, one may recriminate and condemn oneself for not having answered one remark in a certain way. This is unproductive and unrewarding and should be avoided; at the least verbalize them aloud and have done with them.

There is no sin in having a meal before practice. It should be tried at least once. The realization will develop that it does not conduce to alertness or vigilance or enthusiasm to practice. In this way, one should examine a number of possibilities that are existent in one's environment and daily life, with a view to determining their value or otherwise.

Sex is another topic that for some people may prove to be a disturbing factor to the ease of concentration. I rather agree with Crowley in this respect: that there will be little or no clear thinking on this topic until sex is recognized as a branch of athletics or erotology and not in the least bit related to ethics and morality. Informed common sense, and familiarity with some of the more liberal views held by modern psychologists and sociologists will go far towards handling this subject.

Religious Devotion

This is another topic raised as being a necessary preliminary to the practice of meditation. But nowadays this is less of a necessity than ever it was in years gone by. An agnostic or atheist can practise meditation just as successfully and as effectively as the person who prays for help to God, or who constantly affirms, in true metaphysical fashion, that all distractions are out of harmony with the essential being of God. By pleading for the Grace of God, he believes concentration may be more easily come by. *Religious attitudes are more meaningful and productive as a result of the mystical experience achieved by the practice of meditation than those compulsively assumed before hand as a theoretical aid to meditation.* The practices produce their own mystico-religious results that the agnostic and atheist can benefit by and proceed accordingly. Prior beliefs are in effect worthless, unless accompanied by profound conviction, deep emotion and fervour.

This is not to assume that a genuinely religious person may not sincerely use his faith and his devotions to further his religious practices and concentration. I do not question this sincerity. However, I must confess that I have found it to be relatively rare. The agnostic position may prove more fruitful. Objectivity can be a tremendous asset in this connection.

Introspection

One of the succeeding stages is introspection. I can only liken this to what is known in psychoanalysis as free association. One simply lets the mind wander, letting it move where it will, without hindrance. One simply watches. It is like putting a horse out to pasture, without rope or saddle or any other hindrance to block its free movement. In this practice, one rapidly proves for oneself a basic theorem of psychoanalysis, that all thoughts are strictly determined. One discovers soon enough that one can trace all thoughts to a causative chain that extends far back into the past. But this has to be self-discovered.

'Until you know what the mind is doing you cannot control it.' So wrote Swami Vivekananda many years ago, and what he said then is still true.

Give it the full length of the reins; many hideous thoughts may come into it; you will be astonished that it was possible for you to think such thoughts. But you will find that each day the mind's vagaries are becoming less and less violent, that each day it is becoming calmer. In the first few months you will find that the mind will have a thousand thoughts, later you will find that it is toned down to perhaps seven hundred, and after a few more months it will have fewer and fewer, until at last it will be under perfect control, but we must patiently practise every day. As soon as the steam is turned on the engine must run, and as soon as things are before us we must perceive; so a man, to prove that he is not a machine, must demonstrate that he is under the control of nothing.

Using a Tape Recorder

A favourite device of mine at one time was to use a wire recorder during each session of practice. I suggest that the instrument be so prepared that it will run for a full hour without needing any attention from the student. This is not to state that at the beginning any one practice session should run for an hour. On the contrary: it is my contention that practice sessions initially should be relatively short – not more than ten minutes at a time. One could practise once, twice, or even three times a day. As time goes on, and as proficiency is gained, then the time could be extended considerably. But the recorder should be able to handle a full hour's recording in the event of one getting carried away by the process.

Incidentally, one should determine beforehand how long each session should be. If it is for ten minutes, then one could set an alarm clock, or a kitchen timer for that length of time. Once it has sounded off, the practice should be stopped promptly. In this way, one will not be carried away over-enthusiastically by recording the associations that occur to one during the practice of introspection.

The Hidden Content of Consciousness

While sitting upright and motionless in the meditative position, quietly verbalize to the microphone nearby any thought, memory, idea, sensation or feeling that happens to arise. If there is a second practice period during the same day, or if there is some open time available, the recording could be played back so that one may hear audibly what one has been previously thinking.

Usually, the results are shocking as well as illuminating. It will give the student an idea of what lies concealed within his psyche. They are shocking only if one has been wholly honest in overtly verbalizing the stray forbidden thoughts that occasionally float before the inner vision. The development of some mental honesty is a tremendous gain.

Once one has really become aware of the hidden content of consciousness and struggled to come to terms with oneself, the inner conflicts produced by the censorship of the super ego (conscience) is considerably reduced, and so will be the number of 'breaks' in concentration produced by the forcible pressure of these repressed ideational and emotional contents within the psyche.

Draining Off Mental Energy

The practice of introspection, free association recording, and playback should be pursued for many months until the shock and dismay usually experienced at the hideous thinking one is capable of has been dissipated or reduced to practically zero. Then one is ready to attack the process of concentration directly.

Directly? I think not. The head-on attack of forcing the mind by an act of will to concentrate on a single object or symbol, while admirable in intent, is misguided from the *tactical* point of view. In the end, this kind of tactic results in a shadow-boxing type of reaction. The greater the effort of will to force concentration upon the mind, the greater is the reaction in terms of mind-wandering, plain resistance, and feelings of fatigue and exhaustion.

I have never forgotten a remark made by a teacher of mine when I was a boy in early grade school. He said there are more ways of killing a dog than by choking it with butter. And there are many ways of learning how to concentrate than by trying to bludgeon the mind into obedience, and turning it into a most unwilling and resistant instrument.

One important contribution to the subject of concentration is the demand that we consider the mind as a piece of machinery, intricate and infinitely complex, but a piece of machinery nonetheless. And, as such, it should never be forgotten that machinery requires energy in order to run. Now if it were possible to drain off the energy from this machinery, or to redistribute it in some manner, the machinery would stop running. So far so good.

Now throughout history, this notion having been often considered, various devices have been employed to drain off the energy from the machinery of the mind. Starvation or a restricted diet has been one method. However, this merely ruins the body as such, so that nothing much can be done apart from nursing a sick and malfunctioning physical organism; and in any event, such devices stimulate the mind into tremendous bursts of fantasy about food, banquets and gluttonous debauches so that some of the ancients complained bitterly that they were being tormented by the Devil and all his hosts.

Flagellation has been used to whip the body into submission in the hope that at the same time the mind will also be beaten into submission and give up its incessant wandering. This is a forlorn hope. Usually anyone crass enough to attempt these austerities has a secret or unconscious yen for masochistic indulgence, and the derivation of pleasure in some form from the whipping stimulates the mind into further pleasurable anticipation of repeat performances. No energy is, in fact, drained off.

Hair shirts, abstaining from bathing and so becoming lice-ridden, standing or sitting in one posture for long periods of time and other forms of mortification to give affront to the vanity of the mind yield absolutely nothing. They simply turn the entire process of learning to concentrate into a nightmare and a devilish ordeal.

Depriving the mind of sensory stimuli by solitary confinement is one way of turning off the current, but then one has to be prepared to face the uprush of proprioceptive stimuli from the muscles and organs of the body, and the appearance of hallucinations and unconsciously derived imagery and fantasy. None of this seems, in any way, to rob the mind of its energy. On and on it goes, endlessly perpetuating thoughts and fantasies and memories, all designed, apparently, by a malignant power to interfere with the development of concentration.

Some of the Eastern experts in the process of meditation call attention to the fact that sustained or prolonged meditation will certainly evoke specific hallucinations, which they call *maya*. These hallucinations are nothing but the outcropping and projection of the latent contents of the unconscious. They must be recognized as such otherwise it is said that there is danger to the stability of the psyche.

Mantras

Earlier, I made mention of the fact that a strong emotion or a powerful physical sensation will induce a species of concentration spontaneously. There is no draining off of energy, however, but it might be possible to use the foregoing methods with a third one that will simultaneously induce concentration and circulate the energy away from the mind itself. We have, then, three topics to dilate on: emotion, sensation, and circulation of energy.

Prior to dealing with these three ideas directly, however, there is one more issue to be enlarged on, since it bears indirectly on them. There is, traditionally, a simple device having as its intent the slowing down of the quicksilver-like movement of the mind in all directions at once. It is known as a mantra. Apart from all other considerations, a mantra is simply a word or a phrase, usually of a sacred or religious import, which is repeated over and over again, either audibly or subvocally, but more often mentally, until after some days it is taken up by the mind itself. In that case, it goes on repeating itself automatically. Thus, a mechanical type of concentration is acquired that can then be used to further the pre-determined goals.

There are Eastern mantras and Western affirmations. There is little to choose between them. Only your own preference or prejudice is the crucial factor to be considered. Some of the classical Eastern ones are: *Om Tat Sat! Tat Twam Asi; Om nimaha shivaya om; Om mani padme hum.* Regardless of what their literal meanings may be, they take on another meaning altogether after their repetition has become an automatic process. Insights dawn spontaneously.

Metaphysical mantras, based upon Christianity, are most common: 'The Lord is my Shepherd, I shall not want' has achieved a wide popularity, with some other phrases extrapolated from the Scriptures.

A mantra taken from the Catholic missal is also very effective: *Kyrie eleison. Christe eleison.* This same missal may be used to indicate many more similarly effective ones. The equivalent of one of these phrases from the Russian Orthodox Church *Gospody polmilui* is

most euphonious and makes for a good rhythmic mantra. The Eastern
Church has a melodious hymn sung on Good Friday consisting only
of these two words, sung over and over again in a most effective
manner.

'Lord Jesus Christ, Son of God, have mercy on me a poor sinner.'
This is a Christian mantra that has been described very poignantly in
The Way of a Pilgrim, a book every student should read. It is about a
simple Russian peasant who wanted to discover the meaning and
method of the Biblical injunction 'to pray without ceasing' and 'to
pray with the heart'.

I must quote the following passage from this book, for it is so naive,
sincere and so technically superb that it cannot help being useful:

> Picture to yourself your heart in just the same way, turn your eyes
> to it just as though you were looking at it through your breast, and
> picture it as clearly as you can. And with your ears listen closely to
> its beating, beat by beat. When you have got into the way of doing
> this, begin to fit the words of the Prayer to the beats of the heart
> one after the other, looking at it all the time. Thus, with the first
> beat, say or think 'Lord', with the second, Jesus', with the third,
> 'Christ', with the fourth, 'have mercy', and with the fifth, 'on me'.
> And do it over and over again. This will come easily to you, for you
> already know the groundwork and the first part of praying with the
> heart.

In the book, the pilgrim is describing the method to a blind man
who had previously become familiar with the Russian mystical classic
The Philokalia.

> Afterwards, when you have grown used to what I have just told
> you about, you must begin bringing the whole Prayer of Jesus into
> and out of your heart in time with your breathing, as the Fathers
> taught. Thus, as you draw your breath in, say, or imagine yourself
> saying, 'Lord Jesus Christ', and as you breathe out again, 'have
> mercy on me'. Do this as often and as much as you can, and in a
> short space of time you will feel a slight and not unpleasant pain in
> your heart, followed by a warmth. Thus by God's help you will get
> the joy of self-acting inward prayer of the heart.

Joel Goldsmith gives several of these modern metaphysical
affirmations in his excellent book *The Art of Meditation*, which should
certainly appear on any list of worthwhile books on the topic of
meditation. And of course we must never forget the famous book of

Mary Baker Eddy, which became the backbone of the Christian Science Movement. 'God is All in all. God is good. God is mind God, Spirit, being all, nothing is matter.' The whole of this dogmatic statement (or only parts of it) was used as affirmation, with the intent of turning one's mind in an act of concentration to God for the healing of bodily or mental ills and wants. The New Thought movement, which has evolved by devious routes from the mainstream of Christian Science, has likewise devised hundreds of new affirmations. The little magazines published by the Unity organization sometimes give a different affirmation for every day of the week or month, as aids to meditation.

The Mohammedans have a long sonorous Arabic mantra, which for pure euphony has much to recommend it: *Qol; Hua Allahu achad; Allahu Assamad; lam yalid walam yulad; walam yakun lahu kufwan achad.* Translated into English, which has little to do with the efficiency of a mantra, it means: 'Say, He is God alone! God the Eternal! He begets not and is not begotten! Nor is there like unto Him any one!'

Another affirmation or mantra having its roots in ancient magico-religious traditions is 'There is no part of me which is not of the Gods.' Originally it was part of one of the rituals in the Egyptian *Book of the Dead*. In the middle of the nineteenth century it was appropriated by the Hermetic Order of the Golden Dawn, one of whose chiefs, MacGregor Mathers, used it as a greeting to whomsoever he met.

Crowley's mantra from *The Book of the Law* also has a sonorous rhythm. He transliterated this from an Egyptian stele in the Boulak Museum: *A ka dua. Tuf ur biu. Bi aa chefu. Dudu ner af an nuteru.* His poetic rendering of this is given as:

> Unity uttermost showed!
> I adore the might of Thy breath,
> Supreme and terrible God,
> Who makes the Gods and Death
> To tremble before Thee: –
> I, I adore Thee!

One of the famous Buddhist mantras is: *Namo tasso Bhagavato Arahato Samma-sambuddhasa.* Its meaning is: 'Hail unto Thee, the Blessed One, the Perfected One, the Supremely Enlightened One.'

There are many others. It only remains for the student to select the one that he is attracted towards, and for which he feels some sympathy. It really would not matter what its nature was. For example, consider the following: 'Hey diddle diddle. The cat and the fiddle. The cow jumped over the moon.' Were he to feel that he could readily seize upon this prosaic nursery rhyme, repeating it over and over again, it would serve for the student just as effectively as any other mantra.

Practising with a Mantra

Whatever it is, select a mantra that suits you – and then start practising. I suggest that at the outset it be repeated audibly. Only later, as familiarity with the procedure grows, should it be transferred to the psyche to be repeated silently or mentally.

My own predilection is in the area of the Qabalah. A mantra I have often used is *Eheieh*, the divine name attributed to *Kether* the first *Sephirah* or emanation on The Tree of Life. In the past I have often visualized a large Hebrew letter, *Shin*, in bold red outlines above the crown of the head, while continuously vibrating this single word. On other occasions I have used *Achath Ruach Elohim chayim* which means 'One (is she) the Spirit of the Everliving God.' The meaning, however, is subordinate to the continued vibration of the name and to training the mind to take it up spontaneously. This sounds difficult – as does the whole business of practice in this area. But once one has achieved a steady discipline, it is far less difficult than anticipated. Probably the most difficult part of the entire project is simply to make up one's mind to begin, and then sticking to it. Once this initial resistance is overcome, the mastery of a mantra is, actually, relatively easy.

If the student happens to be a religiously-minded person – regardless of his denomination, which is not particularly important to this issue – the use of a mantra can be infinitely rewarding. The repetition of the phrase – be it from the Psalms, the Gospels, the Koran, the Vedas, or even the *Book of the Dead* – is accompanied by the emergence of a great deal of effect. The sincerely devout Jewish Qabalist who repeats the ancient prayer 'Hear O Israel: the Lord our God, the Lord is One' is investing this sentence with a tremendous amount of energy and emotion. *It is this passion that directs the mind one-pointedly towards the maintenance of the repetition, until concentration is obtained.* And so with the orthodox Catholic who, like the hero of *The Way of the Pilgrim*, repeats fervently 'O Lord Jesus Christ, Son of God, have mercy upon me a poor sinner.' The loading of emotion on to the mechanical repetition of the mantra forces the recalcitrant mind to behave, inducing a deep state of concentration. With practice, the concentration can be turned on and off until it becomes a faculty that is as readily available as is the electric current in the modern home.

Mantras for Atheists or Agnostics

The agnostic or atheist who has no religious feeling *per se*, and who thus will not be emotionally moved by the more conventional religious mantras, can nonetheless still avail himself of the distinct benefits to be obtained by employing emotion as a tool. He could select some phrase from a poem or a novel of any kind that has moved him profoundly – and I am certain this has happened at some time to almost everybody – and then use this as his own mantra. Failing this, he could fall back on some personal private experience, such as the courting of a lover in early adolescent days when emotion ran high. And picturing this lover in mind, he could repeat over and over again, as if it were a religious mantra, 'Darling, I love you! Darling, I love you!' and if this combination of mental picture and repeated phrase can evoke the deep emotion that was felt long years anterior to practice, it will succeed no less than the religiously oriented mantra in developing concentration.

The First Stage

'What is meant by holding the mind to certain points?' asks Vivekananda in his excellent book *Raja Yoga*. 'Forcing the mind to feel certain parts of the body to the exclusion of others. For instance, try to feel only the hand, to the exclusion of other parts of the body. When the *Chitta*, or mind-stuff, is confined and limited to a certain place, this is called *Dharana*. This *Dharana* is of various sorts, and along with it, it is better to have a little play of the imagination. For instance, the mind should be made to think of one point in the heart. That is very difficult; an easier way is to imagine a lotus there. That lotus is full of light, effulgent light. Put the mind there.'

Breathing

The next stage is to practise simple rhythmic breathing. The simplicity of this method is its great advantage. It consists of inhaling slowly to a certain count, and exhaling to the same count. If one's chest is tight muscularly, then one should be guided accordingly to select a short rhythm (such as 1, and 2, and 3, and 4) and then exhale to the same rhythm. It is my suggestion to include 'and' between every number so as to slow down the counting process. This is most important. For not only does the establishment of the rhythm produce some perceptible physical results, but at the same time the gradual extension of the rhythm results in the slowing down of mental activity. As the muscular tensions are released, longer rhythms may be used.

The development of the rhythm sooner or later sets up well-defined physical sensations, largely of two kinds – though this is not to say that there are not many others. The first is the experiencing of a tingling sensation all over the body. It can easily be likened to that sensation when one has been pressing on a limb and the circulation has been initially cut off for a few seconds. When the pressure is removed, a prickling sensation is experienced as the blood circulation is restored. Rhythmic breathing initiates an analogous sensation in every cell throughout the entire body.

Parallel with this is a peculiar rippling sensation very hard to describe that is experienced in the diaphragmatic segment of the thorax. As it becomes established by persisting with the rhythmic breathing it tends to spread widely, until there is a well-defined feeling of a total bodily pulsation. These have to be experienced to fully appreciate the nature of this description. Finally, these sensations are accompanied by pleasant feelings. Some describe them as 'soft', 'melting', 'delicious'.

These extraordinary and unusual feelings are but the harbingers of the ineffable bliss and ecstasy that, one day, will occur as the later spiritual results unfold. 'The body is weary, and the soul is sore weary, but ever abides the sure consciousness of ecstasy, unknown, yet known in that its being is certain. O Lord, be my helper and bring me to the bliss of the beloved!'

The Power of Rhythm

The experience of a pleasant emotional response no matter how gentle or light to the rhythmic breathing, will go a long way towards facilitating a state of concentration. With the process eliciting pleasure there will be less tendency for the mind to wander – except to other and former experiences when pleasure was the keynote. There is likely to be some mind-wandering on purely pleasurable experiences. But however much wandering there is, it represents the beginning of some concentration on one particular topic.

Furthermore, the experience of a definite physical sensation or a diaphragmatic rippling will be very heartening and encouraging to the beginner. It will comprise another aid to focusing the mind on a single point – in this case, the breathing process itself. Having to count mentally in order to establish the rhythm also conduces to concentration. A mechanical aid in this direction is a metronome. Listening to the loud clicking, and timing one's breathing in coordination with the sound, is a still further aid to concentration.

Nor is this all. It has long been known that mental hyperactivity is somehow tied to respiratory rapidity. If we are mentally disturbed or excited, the breathing tends to become rapid. This would suggest, then, that if we slow down the rate of respiration to an easy rhythmic rate, the mind's furious turbulence follows suit and can be controlled, so that then, after you have become accustomed to breathing to a simple rhythm of, let us say, four in and four out, the rate can be changed to four in and eight out. Again, the word 'and' should be inserted between each number so as to prevent the likelihood of hurry. Above all, strain should be avoided. Here the good sense of the student has to be called upon. If he has a more experienced friend or fellow-student who can act in this instance as an authoritative teacher, he will see that the student does not hurry or strain while striving for a prolonged rhythm.

Fascinating the Mind

As skill and ease are obtained, the rhythm can be changed in a variety of ways: first, to prevent boredom, which is an ever-present enemy, and second, because the different sensations engineered by a different rhythm, will have the effect of fixing the mind upon them. In other words, *the sensations themselves facilitate concentration.*

I cannot stress this notion too strongly. In my experience, it is most important and I do not feel that this has been stressed sufficiently by modern authorities who, I am sure, know a good deal more about concentration and meditation than I do. Initially, I obtained the clue from two classical books on Yoga – *The Hatha Yoga Pradipika* and *The Shiva Sanhita*. Both of them describe a whole variety of bizarre practices with which we are not in the least bit concerned. But as I read them, years ago, I noticed a phrase common to both: that when the sounds of the Nada occur (The Voice of the Silence, as Blavatsky puts it) – sounds that are internally elicited as certain practices are performed – the mind becomes fascinated by them, being drawn to them irresistibly in much the same way as a bird is irresistibly fascinated by the steady gaze of a snake.

This description stayed with me for many years, until in the course of considerable experimentation with breathing processes – as part of preparation for meditation, and, later, as an operational tool of the Reichian system of psychotherapy – I suddenly joined them together. For I found that these breathing processes, even on a superficial level, without having progressed to the point of eliciting the sounds of the Nada, brought about a variety of somatic and visceral sensations. These kept me utterly fascinated so that wool-gathering was the last thing in the world that could occur. And then, as the years wore on, it occurred to me that this could be used as an operational tool in the development of concentration. In other words, *concentration followed spontaneously and inevitably as the breathing practice produced massive sensory responses.*

Effect of Prolonged Concentration

A most interesting phenomenon may be observed as the outcome of this. If, for example, a series of curious tingling and prickling sensations are initiated in the feet, one's attention becomes automatically drawn to that area. Concentration on the feet develops. The first effect of this concentration is that the sensations become, gradually, enormously heightened. The feet feel alive, buzzing, suffused with electrical energy, or so it seems. This may continue for some considerable time.

Now if the concentration persists on that one spot, unwaveringly and steadfastly, then something happens for which one is totally unprepared. The tingling continues – but a sense of numbness in the feet makes its appearance. Gradually, all awareness of the feet fades out entirely. This is altogether paradoxical. The feet feel alive and vital but at the same time there is no direct awareness of feet. In other words, a basic law evolves out of this. If concentration is prolonged, then sensation becomes almost entirely expunged. The feet disappear from consciousness.

If one were concentrating on sensations in the nose, shortly one would have no awareness of nose at all. It would disappear from view altogether. One might have to open one's eyes and look in a mirror, or bring one's hand up to one's face in order to ascertain whether the nose is still there.

A method that bears some resemblance to this is to be found within Zen Buddhism of the Soto sect. It recommends a meditation practice, 'This very body is Buddha.' When persisted in, psychological phenomena occur of the type referred to above, for the awareness of the body disappears to be replaced by another kind of awareness. This, when meditated upon, is also expunged in very much the same way.

Displacing the Ego

This finding is fraught with the most serious and important consequences when treading the Path. It is axiomatic in most branches of mysticism and occultism, that the ego – or the conscious mind, or the cortex of the brain – is the 'dragon in the way'. 'The mind is the slayer of the Real. Let the disciple slay the slayer.' That is to say, it is the obstacle to realizing that God is here and now, that there is in reality no separation between man and Nature, or between any one soul and the entire universe. This unity has existed from time immemorial and will continue to exist in all time to come. It is only the limitations of our thinking, of our surface consciousness fed by stimuli from the senses, that blind us to the reality of the omnipresence and immanence of God. The 'heresy of separateness' is essentially a product of the ego. It is not a fact in nature.

If therefore the ego can be pushed out of the way by one device or another, then we could become conscious, or we could *realize* as factual, the unity of all of life. In sleep the ego is displaced, but so is the perceiver; in drunkenness the ego is eclipsed – and the perceiver is too; in concentration one disciplines oneself to be able to constrain all thinking to one point – and then ultimately to drop it altogether. In other words, this training is devised so that one can stop thinking, at will, and to resume thinking, when it is necessary to return to one's daily affairs, also at will. When thinking is suspended in this manner, but maintaining vigilance and conscious awareness, then this is enlightenment. God is! It was always thus, and will always be thus. It remained only to get the ego out of the way.

When considering the law of concentration that we are discussing, it becomes clear that if all the attention were concentrated upon the ego itself, at first such an ego-awareness might be extraordinarily heightened. It would appear as if one had a hypertrophied ego, an egomania. But were the concentration to be prolonged, then gradually this egomania would subside and eventually fade out of view entirely. It would leave only an actively empty mind – paradox that this may seem to be – that is acutely conscious of being at one with God and Love and Life and Beauty.

If we must give names to the goals of The Great Work, the development of concentration and meditation, then we have them here: to become acutely aware of one's essential identity with the root and source of life itself, and to become a conscious agency for its continuous activity. Egotism rooted in the self becomes universally enlarged to include the Self of All, because That is All there is. Meditation on the Hindu mantra will disclose this to be the meaning of *Tat Tvam Asi.*

To arrive at this exalted mystical consciousness, which is the goal of all systems of enlightenment, Eastern or Western, we have to become adepts in the utilization of concentration and meditation. And this is why we are discussing ways and means of developing techniques that lead to its mastery.

Hyperventilation

There is a physiological sequel called hyperventilation that we simply must call attention to here. Without it there is simply no understanding of what transpires in some of the more advanced uses of the respiratory technique. What happens as one goes on breathing, with longer periods of exhalation, and longer periods of pause, between exhalation and inhalation, is that most of the carbon dioxide within the alveoli of the lungs is blown off, and greater quantities of oxygen are taken in.

(I must insist, for the sake of the readers who have done some reading on the topic of Yoga and meditation, that there is no alternate nostril-breathing recommended here in this essay. There are no gymnastics, occult or physiological, in these simple exercises to train for meditation. I have nothing but respect for Yoga and pranayama. But this process is not being dealt with here. Both nostrils are kept open. The hands are kept relaxed in the lap, and not brought to the face to open or close one or other of the nostrils.)

The result of taking in an excess of oxygen leads to an extraordinary sequence of events that has been noted and recorded by physiologists. Most of them have only observed it as a pathological process. It remained for Wilhelm Reich, the psychiatrist and one-time disciple of Freud, to realize that it could be used as an operational tool in psychotherapy; and, modestly, it has been left for me to note that it may be used as a tool for the induction of concentration.

With the inhalation of an excess of oxygen – or with the blowing off of residual carbon dioxide, which is saying the same thing – a chemical change is engineered in the blood-stream, rendering it more alkaline. This, in turn, alters the chemical environment of the brain, so that its essential function is changed. What happens is analogous to stating that the individual becomes drunk, not on alcohol, but on oxygen. The normal flow of thoughts, feelings, and bodily function becomes considerably altered, and the individual, unless he is prepared beforehand by instructions such as this, may be inclined to think he is 'out of the groove'. He *is* actually shaken out of his normal dull kind of functioning, and a wide variety of sensations, physical, emotional, and mental are induced.

The only somatic sequel that he needs to be somewhat on guard against is tetany. This represents tonic spasms, stiffnesses developing in different sets of muscles throughout the body. These differ with each person, because each person has his own peculiar set of muscular tensions that is related to his own individual history and emotional background. *The hyperventilation merely intensifies the muscular tensions already existent, to the point where tetany may occur.*

This phenomenon has been long noted in Yoga literature where it is mentioned that at certain stages of development 'automatic rigidity' may occur, and the body may hop around like a frog. With traditional Yoga breathing or pranayama, this is indeed likely to occur, and it represents a distinct piece of personal progress. With the kind of breathing described in this essay, tetany is almost impossible – save perhaps in a very small minority of shallow-breathers, with a hysterical character-structure, who are also sensitive to a surplus of oxygen. The average student to whom this essay is addressed is unlikely to practise for hours at a time, nor to adopt the pranayama technique peculiar to Hatha-Yoga practice. So there is nothing to fear on this score. There is no danger here whatsoever.

In the event that a slight hint of tetany does occur, the breathing technique should be momentarily discontinued, and the respiration permitted to resume its normal pattern while one busies oneself with purely routine prosaic tasks. If this is not adequate, then obtain a large brown paper bag, and breath into it. In this manner, one inspires one's own carbon dioxide, quickly rendering the blood more acid, in which case the tetany, due to over-alkalinization, will disappear. More often than not, it will ease up by itself without anything being done about it.

The only significant symptoms that we need to mention here are: the development of powerful tinglings all over the body, a delightful feeling of relaxation of muscular tensions, dizziness and lightheadedness, pulsations of energy flowing from head to toe, feelings of considerable pleasure, and sensations of quivering and inner trembling which eventually produce a wonderful sense of ease and release.

Hyperventilation sometimes engineers affective discharge, so that one may feel inclined either to laugh almost hysterically, or to break down and dissolve in tears. Should either of these phenomena occur there is no need for alarm. Merely regard them as distinct stages of progress that result in the discharge of repressed emotions and feelings, and realize that once these feelings have been released, the ability to concentrate is enormously enhanced.

Koans

These, however, are the crucial moments, (just when the function of the brain and central nervous system have undergone radical change), when one should employ every known device to *aspire* eagerly and enthusiastically to the highest. The prayers of old-time or magical invocations or the modern-day affirmations will now prove to be pre-eminently useful. Mantras intitiated at this point will be taken up *sua sponte* and act almost as though they were Zen *koans*.

What is a *koan*? According to most authorities, the *koan* is, in effect, not a puzzle to be cleverly solved by an agile monkey-mind; nor is it merely a psychological device to shift or shock the previously fragile ego of a student into a newer species of equilibrium. Certainly it is not a paradox, save to those who have never perceived it from within. It is, however, a simple, clear and direct statement issuing from a specific state of consciousness that it has helped to elicit.

An affirmation or invocation, hence, engaged in at this particular point of development, will exalt the student to the highest state of spiritual consciousness that he is then capable of reaching. Its use may help to precipitate the enlightenment towards which he has been working for so long. It is like placing an arrow in a taut bow. When the cord is released, the arrow is shot with force to its mark. 'I have aimed at the peeled wand of my God, and I have hit; yea, I have hit.'

Suspension of Breath

Having spoken of full breathing and hyperventilation, I should make mention, briefly, of another phenomenon which is the diametrical opposite. When some of the higher results of meditation appear, the breathing sometimes appears to become almost wholly suspended. In reality, it is a very light, fine breathing, existing as it were under the diaphragm – often called interior breathing – which has been nicely described by the ancient Taoists as being 'like the breathing of the infant in the womb.'

Further Breathing Techniques

There is an age-old variation of breathing technique which is exquisite in its simplicity, and miraculous in its effect. No rhythm is deliberately set up in the breathing process. No attempt is made to regulate it in any way. One merely breathes in a natural ordinary way. But as one does, one simply notes 'The breath flows in. The breath flows out.' And that is all. It sounds so simple, and basically it is.

In so doing, one may become exquisitely aware of the nostrils, against which the incoming tide of air hits; then, after a while, of the turbinates, the upper portions of the nose; later, of the throat and then of the bronchial tree and the lungs themselves. It might be worth while to imagine the air, incoming and outgoing, as a white mist that one is capable of observing and tracing. And as one does all this, lo! and behold! One is concentrating.

Finally, as a result of these breathing practices and the acquisition of concentration, one may become aware of the fact that one is becoming enormously vitalized. The impression is that of being saturated with cosmic energy that flows through every cell and pore of one's being. At this stage of practice, one needs to learn to circulate the energy – and in this way, to return to a theme of an earlier page – to drain out the energy from the mind. When this kind of skill has been achieved, one merely has to think and lightly will that energy to move and of course it moves. There are several methods of circulation.

Circulation of Energy

The ancient Qabalistic approach is to concentrate on the crown of the head, imagining this to be the centre of one's spiritual life, which is the Universal Self; and, while so doing, to imagine and will that all the energies in the lower areas of the body are gradually being pulled up, sucked up as it were, to the light above the crown of the head. Persistency is required, practice being engaged in day after day. One of these days, while working, so Vitvan says, there is an inner explosion, the electrical circuit is, as it were, completed, and illumination occurs. One *knows*. Not with a knowing of the brain or mind, but with a realization of one's divine ancestry and divine nature — the goal of all mystical work, and the beginning of spiritual freedom.

The full method is rather more detailed, and is described at some length in the essay *The Art of True Healing* (see p. 137). It consists basically of the visualization of five centres within the organism and the vibration of certain Qabalistic names within those centres. This develops or releases vast quantities of energy that are circulated in a variety of ways until the organism is enclosed within a vast spinning sphere of light-energy.

A similar method of circulation was once employed by the Chinese Taoists of long ago. The student who is interested should consult Richard Wilhelm's translation of an ancient Chinese text included in Jung's *Secret of the Golden Flower*.

Once this stage is reached, as a result of upright posture and simple breathing and mantra practice, the achievement of concentration at will has become a fact. From this point on, some of the classical practices can be instituted because through them the attainment of the mystical experience becomes a possibility. Call it Union with God, or the discovery of the Inner Self, or the realization of the Buddha-nature, this is the goal to be aimed at once concentration is a faculty that has been developed.

Visualization of Objects

Perfectly prosaic objects can be taken, visualized and concentrated upon. For example, here is one classical set of instructions for *Dharana*, the control of thought, which could be most useful at this particular stage:

1. Constrain the mind to concentrate itself upon a single simple object imagined.

The five tatvas are useful for this purpose: they are: a black oval; a blue disk; a silver crescent; a yellow square; a red triangle.

2. Proceed to combination of simple objects; e.g. a black oval within a yellow square, and so on.

3. Proceed to simple moving objects, such as a pendulum swinging, a wheel revolving, etc. Avoid living objects.

4. Proceed to combinations of moving objects, e.g. a piston rising and falling while a pendulum is swinging. The relation between the two movements should be varied in different experiments.

Or even a system of flywheels, eccentrics, and governor.

5. During these practices the mind must be absolutely confined to the object determined upon; no other thought must be allowed to intrude upon the consciousness. The moving systems must be regular and harmonious.

6. Note carefully the duration of the experiments, the number and nature of the intruding thoughts, the tendency of the object itself to depart from the course laid out for it, and any other phenomena which may present themselves. Avoid overstrain; this is very important.

The Use of Hypnotism

One more approach needs to be considered. This concerns the cooperation of another trained person. It seems to me that hypnotic suggestion in the hands of a reliable teacher trained in meditation could be enormously valuable. It does not eliminate the need for discipline and prolonged practice. Not by any means. But it may make the achievement of discipline and practice easier for some types of students.

There is no reason why, if the student is found to be suggestible, the meditation teacher should not arrange several hypnotic sessions in which some basic notions are laid down. It could be suggested (once the elementary and preliminary hypnotic induction has been found to be effective) that the student should practise daily. A previous discussion should have determined how often and when the student could practise and whether he wishes to do so. Then the number of practices will be carefully stated during hypnosis, and the length of time to be devoted for each practice period. The teacher could then wait for some considerable time to see whether the student was cooperating, or responding to the hypnotic suggestions.

If there is a reasonable response, then the hypnotic suggestions could be extended. For example, suggestions could be given that henceforth the student will find it easy, at the practice period at such and such a time, morning, noon and/or evening, to concentrate all his mental powers on a series of pre-arranged topics, symbols, or concepts. It may require considerable emphasis and repetition for these suggestions to become effective; but there is no reason on earth why they should not become effective.

The usual argument against this kind of technical approach is that it eliminates the student's personal responsibility; that it is not self-induced and self-devised. This argument is altogether without foundation. The student is still obliged to practise, and practise hard and faithfully. He will have discussed with his teacher what should and should not be suggested in hypnosis, and has given his entire assent to the procedure. But it is still his mind that he has to concentrate, and he will have to devote considerable time and effort to achieve success. Nothing is changed in the traditional procedures, except perhaps that an additional help-incentive or motive has been added.

In this connection, it should always be remembered that all hetero-suggestion becomes, in the last resort, auto-suggestion. It is suggestion given to, and accepted by oneself, but with the aid of a second party.

In one sense, this help has always been recognized. Sometimes the student was permitted to meditate in the company or atmosphere of the teacher. If the student had made a transference to the teacher, or was deeply devoted to him, such a practice had been known to be of considerable service. Sometimes group meditations have been resorted to. It has been theorized that, if a group of students practise together in a meditation hall – as is common within the confines of Zen Buddhism – all benefit enormously by becoming more concentrated more quickly and more easily.

I do not doubt the efficacy of any of these procedures. It is merely my contention that if these are valid, then hypnotic suggestion is also valid and should be used in certain selected cases as a means of disposing of stubborn psychological resistances and obstacles.

I should mention that while performing these exercises of every type, a record should be kept. A book or diary should be maintained just for the purpose of entering up the practices performed, the time of the day, the mood one happened to be in, the kind of weather generally prevailing, and any other conditions that you happen to be aware of that may have some bearing on the experiments performed. Make the record as comprehensive, though not necessarily lengthy, as possible. One day in the future, after some attainment has been reached, this will be seen to have considerable value. And if you are lucky enough to have the guidance of a teacher of any degree or grade, he will want to see the record to know how thorough you may or may not have been.

The Final Union

The instruction quoted above mentioned only the most prosaic of objects to use for constraining the mind to a single point. On the other hand, objects that have a religious or mystical or occult significance more often than not produce results more quickly. And while we are advised to 'work without lust of result', this attitude is the result of, rather than a prerequisite to, the mystical experience. Once one has discovered the God within, the nature of all one's reactions to oneself, one's environment (which is seen to be self-created) and to all else undergoes a massive revolution. One of these changes, of course, is so to function that the fruits of action are of no concern to us. This is Karma Yoga in the true sense of the word. The results are the concern of God, and that is all.

Meditation consists in turning the concentrated mind to any particular topic that requires attention. All the previous discussions were devoted towards developing concentration, without which so-called meditation is merely wool-gathering and uncontrolled fantasy. Meditation based upon concentration eventuates in a union between the meditator and that which is meditated upon, the union of the subject and object, the union of God and Man. Regardless of the language employed to describe it – whether we use Eastern terms such as *Dhyana* and *Samadhi*, or the achievement of *Moksha* or *Mukti* – this is the goal towards which meditation is aimed.

It represents freedom and liberty in the fullest and most philosophical sense of the words. The unity and universality of life, love and beauty are the spiritual components of the enlightenment that is realized with awe, wonder and true simplicity. 'The earth is the Lord's and the fulness thereof'. And since *Tat tvam asi* is seen in meditation to be the truth, the Meditator and the Lord are one.

So to what end, all of this hard work, discipline and constant prayer, this appalling labour to develop concentration? Some of the goals aimed at have been simply described; I doubt if anything is to be gained by a great deal of rhetoric or description of the mystical states sought after or aspired towards. However, to close this essay, I can do no better than to quote, as an example, the illuminations of Jacob Boehme one of the greatest Christian mystics of any age.

Sitting one day in his room, 'his eyes fell upon a burnished pewter dish, which reflected the sunshine with such marvellous splendour that he fell into an inward ecstasy, and it seemed to him as if he could now look into the principles and deepest foundations of things. He believed that it was only a fancy, and in order to banish it from his mind he went out upon the green. But here he remarked that he gazed into the very heart of things, the very herbs and grass, and that actual nature harmonized with what he had inwardly seen. He said nothing of this to anyone, but praised and thanked God in silence.'

Not too long after this initial illumination, 'he was again surrounded by the divine light and replenished with the heavenly knowledge; insomuch as going abroad in the fields to a green before Neys Gate, at Goerlitz, he there sat down and, viewing the herbs and grass of the field in his inward light, he saw into their essences, use and properties, which were discovered to him by their lineaments, figures and signatures. In like manner he beheld the whole creation, and from that foundation he afterwards wrote his book, *De Signatura Rerum.* In the unfolding of those mysteries before his understanding he had a great measure of joy, yet returned home and took care of his family and lived in great peace and silence, scarcely intimating to any these wonderful things that had befallen him.'

FURTHER READING

Art of Meditation, Joel Goldsmith.
Patanjali's Yoga Aphorisms, William Q. Judge.
Science of Breath, Yogi Ramacharaka.
Part One of *Book Four*, Frater Perdurabo (Aleister Crowley).
Concentration and Meditation, Buddhist Lodge (London).
Meditation, Vitvan (School of the Natural Order).
The Zen Koan, Ruth Fuller Sasaki.
Spiritual Exercises, St Ignatius of Loyola.
Man's Highest Purpose, Karel Weinfurter.
The Way of a Pilgrim, translated from the Russian by R.M. French.

4. THE QABALAH OF NUMBER AND MEANING

An Elementary Manual of Numerical Procedures

When I was about sixteen years of age, I first became interested enough in the Qabalah to read voraciously what little of it was available at that time in English. It was surprisingly diminutive in quantity and quality.

Since I then resided in Washington, D.C., I made the Library of Congress my second home. I derived a great deal of pleasure browsing, not only through the extensive files but, after obtaining permission, through the vast stacks also. In due course of time, I had made the acquaintance of the scholarly head of the Semitic Division of the Library and, as though I were free-associating to him, made mention of a burning ambition. When I knew enough, I wanted to be able to translate into English several of the ancient texts that still remained in Hebrew and Aramaic. He was wise enough to recommend to me a Hebrew tutor. This was a young man attending college in Washington who needed some extra funds to facilitate his staying in the city.

Every week, then, for about a year I received a lesson from him. Gradually I learned to read Hebrew fairly fluently, to understand some of the fundamentals of its complex grammar and syntax, and, if the material was sufficiently elementary, to translate it into English passably well. I never persevered long enough to learn to speak the language – which today I regret very much.

But the major result of that year's tutorship was this: though I never succeeded in fulfilling my adolescent dream to translate

Qabalistic texts into English, I did manage to acquire a solid foundation of the language which has stood me in good stead where some Qabalistic fundamentals were concerned.

Gematria, for example, really presents no problem. This I attribute entirely to the linguistic education given me by my tutor, and the same is true for other phases of the so-called practical Qabalah.

Now by this I do not wish to imply that every student should take a year of Hebrew grammar and reading in order to understand some of the Qabalistic methods of elucidation of hidden facets of meaning in the names and symbols of the Old Testament; or to enable him intelligently to construct talismans and amulets in that branch of Qabalah that is known as Theurgy. This is not altogether necessary.

But it may be worthwhile pointing out that great advantage may be obtained from a little study of the Hebrew alphabet, and from some slight experience in drawing and painting these letters as the magical symbols they really are, as well as from familiarizing oneself with certain basic Hebrew words relative to the *Sephiroth* on The Tree of Life. All this would render intelligible numbers of facts which even otherwise astute writers and students of the Qabalah are inclined to gloss over, dismissing them as wholly unimportant to the subject.

Simple Gematria

A few very simple examples should rapidly convey the kind of hidden meaning sought by the Qabalists in their apparently arbitrary manipulation of words, letters and numbers.

For instance, there is the Hebrew word *Achad*. It means 'one' or 'unity'. Its spelling is:

Aleph	+	*Cheth*	+	*Daleth*
1		8		4

Its numerical total or value, or Gematria, thus is thirteen, 13. It so happens that there is another Hebrew word *ahavah* – meaning 'love'. It is spelt:

Aleph	+	*Heh*	+	*Beth*	+	*Heh*
1		5		2		5

Its numerical value is also thirteen, as is the preceding word. Thus it is assumed that, since they have identical number values, there is a connection between love and unity – one leading into and producing the other. I can never think of this matter without recalling St Paul's definition of charity or love:

Though I speak with the tongues of men and angels, and have not charity, I am become as sounding brass, or a tinkling cymbal ... Charity suffereth long, and is kind; charity envieth not; charity vaunteth not itself, is not puffed up, doth not behave itself unseemly, seeketh not her own, is not easily provoked, thinketh no evil, rejoiceth not in iniquity, but rejoiceth in the truth; beareth all things, believeth all things, hopeth all things, endureth all things. Charity never faileth; but whether there be prophecies, they shall fail; whether there be tongues, they shall cease; whether there be knowledge, it shall vanish away. For we know in part, and we prophesy in part. But when that which is perfect is come, then that which is in part shall be done away ... And now abideth faith, hope, charity, these three; but the greatest of these is charity.

If we join the numbers of love and unity together, uniting them as it were, the product becomes 26. This is the numerical value of the Tetragrammaton, the four-lettered name of God:

Yod		*Heh*		*Vav*		*Heh*		
10	+	5	+	6	+	5	=	26

From this operation, the Qabalists therefore deduce that God, who is One and only One, operates through love, and that His nature may well be defined as unity and love conjoined. Or, that He is a unity operating through duality to produce love.

Incidentally, it is worth mentioning that there are two valuable aids for the student who is attempting to become adept in the use of these methods. The first is a Hebrew-English and English-Hebrew Dictionary which he can consult for the meanings of words developed through Gematria. The second is an even more valuable book. It is *Sepher Sephiroth* to be found in *Equinox VIII*. This is a large book originally begun by Frater Iehi Aour (Allan Bennett) of the Golden Dawn, and then continued and completed by Aleister Crowley who became his *chela*, in the early years of this century.

This book consists of a large number of Hebrew words extrapolated both from the Scriptures and from some of the original Qabalistic texts — particularly parts of the *Zohar* and the *Sepher Yetzirah*. The Gematria of several hundreds of words and names have been carefully worked out by these two Qabalists, who then classified each word according to its number. So that if in the course of study one has developed a significant number, it is then possible to look it up in *Sepher Sephiroth* in order to ascertain what other words or names have been gathered together with that particular number.

The more skill one develops in using the Qabalah of numbers

and meaning, the more useful this book becomes. It is really a dictionary of Qabalistic numbers. It has been republished in *The Qabalah of Aleister Crowly*, (N.Y. Weiser and Co., 1973).

	Name in Hebrew	Meaning of Letter	English Letter	Numer- ation	Sepher Yetzirah	Tarot	
1.	Aleph	Ox	A	1		0	– Fool
2.	Beth	House	B	2	Mercury	I	– Magician
3.	Gimel	Camel	G	3	Moon	II	– High Priestess
4.	Daleth	Door	D	4	Venus	III	– Empress
5.	Heh	Window	H	5	Aries	IV	– Emperor
6.	Vav	Nail	V	6	Taurus	V	– Hierophant
7.	Zayin	Sword	Z	7	Gemini	VI	– Lovers
8.	Cheth	Fence	Ch	8	Cancer	VII	– Chariot
9.	Teth	Serpent	T	9	Leo	VIII	– Strength
10.	Yod	Finger	I,J,Y	10	Virgo	IX	– Hermit
11.	Caph	Palm of Hand	K	20	Jupiter	X	– Wheel of Fortune
12.	Lamed	Whip	L	30	Libra	XI	– Justice
13.	Mem	Water	M	40	Water	XII	– Hanged Man
14.	Nun	Fish	N	50	Scorpio	XIII	– Death
15.	Samech	Arrow	S	60	Sagittarius	XIV	– Temperance
16.	Ayun	Eye	NG	70	Capricorn	XV	– Devil
17.	Peh	Mouth	P	80	Mars	XVI	– Blasted Tower
18.	Tzaddi	Hook	TZ	90	Aquarius	XVII	– Star
19.	Qoph	Back of Head	Q	100	Pisces	XVIII	– The Moon
20.	Resh	Head	R	200	Sun	XIX	– The Sun
21.	Shin	Tooth	Sh	300	Fire	XX	– Judgment
22.	Tau	Cross	T	400	Saturn	XXI	– The World

Notariqon

In a quite different direction, there is a method called Notariqon, which is a Hebrew word meaning shorthand writing. It consists in making neologisms (new words) from the initial letters of certain selected words.

In alchemical literature, there is a famous example of the use of

Notariqon. Take the word vitriol, which is sulphur. Each letter of this word becomes the initial of another word forming a sentence of seven words:

V	Visita
I	Interiora
T	Terrae
R	Rectificando
I	Invenies
O	Occultum
L	Lapidem

The entire sentence, then, which is an expension of vitriol, carries with it the meaning of 'Visit or explore the interior or depths of the Earth, and find and rectify the secret Stone.'

One of the traditional names for the Qabalah is the *Chokmah Nestorah*, the Secret Wisdom. It is considered to be that esoteric knowledge which has been handed down from time immemorial. By taking the first letter of these two words, *Cheth* and *Nun*, and combining them, the result is a word pronounced *chen*. By consulting a Hebrew lexicon, it will discovered that there is a legitimate word *chen* which means grace. Hence the Qabalists argued that when it is mentioned in holy script that God vouchsafed His grace to so-and-so, the hidden interpretation is that he transmitted the secret esoteric knowledge of the divine life and plan. This was His grace.

The Notariqon of the Tenach

An even more common and prosaic example of this method is in daily use among the Jewish people, though it is strongly to be doubted if many of them recognize it as a traditional method of Qabalistic exegesis. In Hebrew, the Bible – the Old Testament – is named the *Tenach* (always remember the 'ch' in Hebrew is a gutteral pronunciation, as in the Scottish word 'loch'). It is spelled *Tau, Nun* and final *Caph*.

This is really a notariqon, or a neologism, based upon three Hebrew words:

Torah	– the first few books of the Bible, the so-called Five Books of Moses.
N'vee-im	– the books of the Prophets, several texts including Isaiah, Jeremiah, etc.
K'soovim	– the Holy Writings; the miscellaneous group of scriptures comprised of the Psalms, Proverbs, Ecclesiastes, *et al.*

The first letter of each of these three words is extracted and used to form a new word *Tenach*. This word is, in effect, a shorthand abbreviation to represent the contents of the whole of the Old Testament.

The Gematria of 'Amen'

Another very common word, used by Jews and all Christian denominations alike, without very much insight or understanding, is the word 'Amen'. Its origins and meaning are quite obscure. Its use at the close of a prayer is generally considered to imply 'Let it be so!' or 'So mote it be!' The Qabalists, however, give it an interpretation which is a particular exhortation of divinity. Its letters, *Aleph, Mem, Nun*, are considered to be the initials of the three Hebrew words relating to God.

> *Aleph* = the first letter of *Adonai*, my Lord.
> *Mem* = the first letter of *Melekh*, King.
> *Nun* = the first letter of *Na'amon*, Faithful.

The whole meaning of 'Amen', then, is 'Lord, Faithful King'. The peroration is thus simultaneously a divine invocation.

If we wished to pursue this further, we could determine the Gematria of 'Amen', which is:

$$\left. \begin{array}{l} Aleph = 1 \\ Mem = 40 \\ Nun = 50 \end{array} \right\} \quad = 91.$$

There are a number of other Hebrew words in *Sepher Sephiroth* having this same number. Somehow an intimate connection would have to be established between them. *Ehlon (Aleph, Yod, Lamed, Nun)* is a tree. The biblical word *Ephod (Aleph, Peh, Daleth)* meaning the coloured garment worn by the high priest, has also the same number. *Malkah (Mem, Lamed, Caph, Aleph)* a virgin or a bride, as well as *Manna (Mem, Nun, Aleph)* are still further examples of this number. Connections between these words and numbers may appear obscure at first, but the wise experienced Qabalist could readily trace them out. In reality, a species of free association is used.

There is one final manipulation of 'Amen' and its numerical value of 91. These two digits may be added together by so-called theosophical addition to produce 10. Ten is the number on The Tree of Life of *Malkuth*, the Kingdom, the last of the holy emanations from God, the completion of the chain of numbers, and by the elimination of the zero, the beginning of another sequence of numbers and ideas.

'Ruach Elohim'

Finally, there is the example of *Ruach Elohim*, two Hebrew words mentioned in the opening verses of Genesis referring to the Spirit of God brooding over the waters of creation. A more literal rendition would really be 'The Spirit of the Gods'. The Gematria of these two words joined together is 300, demonstrated as follows:

Ruach =	Resh		Vau		Cheth		
	200	+	6	+	8	=	214

Elohim =	Aleph	Lamed	Heh	Yod	Mem		
	1	+ 30	+ 5	+ 10	+ 40	=	86

Added together they yield 300. (By lopping off the two zeros, this number could be reduced to 3, and 3 is the path of *Gimel*, the Camel, attributed to the Tarot card The High Priestess, who has the title of Priestess of the Silver Star − the path descending from *Kether* above to *Tiphareth* below.)

The letter *Shin* − a three pronged letter − was considered to be the equivalent of these two words, not merely because of the identity of their numbers (which would be enough), but because *Shin* in the *Sepher Yetzirah* was attributed to the element of fire. In many areas of the Old Testament, fire is considerred an attribute of God, indicative of His presence. Later, light became one of these attributes − light and fire being interrelated and interconnected. Thus, one of the old magical exercises associated with visualizing the descent of the divine spirit was to use a concrete symbol − a large fiery red letter *Shin*, imagined above the head. In this connection, I never fail to think of the peroration of one of Crowley's earliest essays:

> Under the stars will I go forth, my brothers, and drink of that lustral dew; I will return my brothers, when I have seen God face to face, and read within those eternal eyes the secret that shall make you free ...
>
> Thus shall we give back its youth to the world, for like *tongues of triple flame* we shall brood upon the Great Deep − Hail unto the Lords of the Groves of Eleusis! (my italics)

One of the early traditions has it that when God uttered *Fiat Lux*, 'Let there be light', he commanded not merely the physical appearance of light and all that it entails, but, so states the ancient wisdom, the emergence of the divine mystery. For light is *Aour* (*Aleph, Vav, Resh* = 207) and *Raz*, (*Resh, Zayin* = 207) meaning mystery.

Thus light in all its manifold significances *is* the divine mystery.

The Qabalist catches glimpses of this mythos in his magical or theurgic working, of a ray of the infinite light.

Zohar means radiance or splendour; thus another reference to light. The radiance of the divine light is reflected in the mysteries of the text of this Qabalistic work. But when these mysteries are cloaked in merely literal theological interpretation, this splendour is obscured and hidden. The literal prosaic meaning was always considered by mystics to be but darkness and obscurity. The esoteric interpretations elicit the *Raz* or mystery as well as the *Zohar* or Splendrous Light that many believe to shine through every line of the sacred scriptures.

Ain Soph Aour is the Infinite Light from which the *Sephiroth* of The Tree of Life have emanated. Thus the light is also, in many more ways than one, the great mysterq without end.

Paradise

There is a good deal of symbolic 'play' with the Hebrew word for paradise – *pardes*, meaning also a garden. Some of the early Qabalists related its letters *Peh, Resh, Daleth, Samech* to the four rivers that in Genesis are said to flow forth from the Garden of Eden. For example in the *Golden Dawn*, one of the early rituals contained the following references:

> The River *Naher* (meaning never-failing waters) flows forth from the Supernal Eden and in *Daath* it is divided into four heads:
> *Pison:* Fire – flowing to *Geburah* where there is Gold.
> *Gihon:* Water – the Waters of Mercy, flowing into *Chesed.*
> *Hiddikel:* Air – flowing into *Tiphareth*
> *Phrath* (Euphrates): Earth – flowing into *Malkuth* ... The River going out of Eden is the River of the Apocalypse, the Waters of Life, clear as crystal proceeding from the Throne, on either side of the Tree of Life, bearing all manner of fruit.

Now compare this set of bare occult dogmas relative to the elements to a far earlier Qabalistic interpretation in which these letters and the Rivers are compared to levels of meaning:

1. *Peh* for *Pison* = literal meaning (*Peshat*).
2. *Resh* for *Remez* = allegorical meaning, and the River *Gihon.*
3. *Daleth* for *Derasha* = talmudic (the sharp and deft) interpretation, and for *Hiddikel.*
4. *Samech* for *Sod* = mystical and innermost meaning, and for *Phrath.*

So that the wisdom derived from not one but multiple levels of meaning and interpretation lead, as it were, to paradise, to illumination.

Names of God

There is a page or so from Francis Barrett's *Magus*, the section on Ceremonial Magic, that is of some consequence here. This book, originally published *circa* 1800, is a hotch-potch of superstitious nonsense and some basic magical information, in about equal proportions. New editions of this book are now available,* and the serious student could do far worse than to obtain a copy, so long as he learns to separate the wheat from the chaff which is copiously and abundantly present. Some of this quotation throws a great deal of light on many of the strange-appearing, almost Hebrew names appearing in some of the old invocations.

The Hebrew in this text is appalling. I imagine many of these mistakes have been inadvertently perpetuated by ignorant copyists. Names are copied by students who knew little or no Hebrew so that after the original copy has passed through a dozen illiterate hands, and undergone as many alterations and mutilations, the final product bears little resemblance to any accurate original, and is to all intents and purposes indecipherable.

I saw this phenomenon within the confines of the Golden Dawn. Some of the students must have copied the Hebrew letters from original manuscripts without any insight or understanding. Their inaccuracies and miscopyings have been perpetuated right down the line to this day. Perhaps it may be said that this makes little difference. But it does imply ignorance above all. And when the making and drawing of all talismans are considered, the Hebrew mistakes as seen in specimens repeated by Barrett and in some old grimoires, are so appalling as to make the talisman meaningless. It would be just as effective (or useless, as the case may be) to inscribe hieroglyphs and lines drawn at random instead of Hebrew letters and sigils.

Instances of this type indicate strongly that the elementary study of basic Hebrew should be made mandatory in whatever sanctuaries of initiation still exist so that, if they teach the Qabalah, the monstrous illiterate errors of former times may never again be repeated.

'God himself, though he be one only essence,' wrote Barrett in the section of his book referred to above, 'yet hath divers names, which expound not his divers essences or deities; but certain properties flowing down from him; by which names he pours down upon us and all his creatures, many benefits ...'

The Magus, Thorsons 1977.

In some of the following examples given by Barrett, I have taken the liberty of eliminating the Hebrew letters and making the appropriate corrections in his transliteration into English.

'*Hua* is another name revealed to Esau, signifying the abyss of Godhead ...' This word means simply 'He', and is attributed to *Kether*. '*Esch* is another name received from Moses, which soundeth fire, and is the name of God: *Na* is to be invoked in perturbations and troubles. There is also the name *Yah*, and the name *Elion* (which is translated "the most high"), and the name *Macom* (this word means "place"), the name *Caphu* ...'

Barrett spells this name *Caphu* with a *Caph, Peh*, and *Beth* which is quite meaningless. I can only assume that the *Beth* was a copyist's mistake for a *Resh*, in which case we would find *Capur* or *Kippur*, meaning 'atonement'. '... and the name *Innon*, and the name *Emeth*, which is interpreted truth, and is the seal of God; and there are two other names *Tzur* ("Rock") and *Aben*, ("stone"), both of these signify a solid work, and one of them expressed the Father with the Son; and many names we have placed in the scale of numbers ...' Barrett then mentions the arts of Notariqon and Gematria by means of which words and numbers are derived, and proceeds:

> In like manner the name *Iaia*, from this verse: *YHVH Alohenu YHVH Achod*, this is, God our God is One God. [In reality it is to be translated, 'Jehovah, our God, Jehovah is One.'] In like manner the name *IaVa*, from this verse: *Iehi Aour, vayehi Aour*, that is 'Let there be Light and there was light' ... and this name *Hacaba* is extracted from this verse, *Ha-Qadesh baruch hua* ('the Holy One, blessed be He') ... These sacred words have not their power in magical operations from themselves, as they are words, but from the occult divine powers working by them in the minds of those who by faith adhere to them.

AGLA and ARARITA

I have omitted a direct quotation from Barrett dealing with two classical words found commonly in some of the older magical rituals because they deserve a somewhat fuller consideration. In the banishing ritual of the Pentagram, now to be found in many publications. there is a four-lettered word AGLA. This is another good example of a notariqon, and its analysis is really quite simple. There are four words from the Scriptures meaning 'Thou art mighty for ever, O Lord [or Adonai].' In Hebrew, this phrase is *Atoh gibor l'olahm adonai*. The initials of these words placed together form AGLA.

There is an even more common ritual name which is more obscure (and which has often been miscopied atrociously), save to the rare good student. The magical name ARARITA is found particularly in the Hexagram Ritual, and is to be vibrated in each of the four quarters while tracing the appropriate geometrical figure with sigils. The six points and the centre of the Hexagram are attributed to the *forces* of the seven planets, which are thus invoked or banished by the correct use of this figure. It, too, is a fine example of a notariqon, and its seven letters are the initials of the following sentece: 'One is His beginning; One is His individuality; His permutation is One.' The corresponding Hebrew is: *Achad raysheethoh; achad Resh Yechidathoh; Temurathoh achod.*

The word *Achad* means 'one'; we have examined this word several times so far. *Raysheeth* is the Hebrew word for beginning, and the addition of the suffix 'oh' merely means 'His'. *Resh* means a head or a beginning, and is the root of *Raysheeth*. Qabalistic students will remember the word *Yechidah* as being attributed to *Kether*, representing, when dealing with the constitution of man the Individual, the immortal part of man. So that the phrase *Resh Yechidathoh* means the Head of his Individuality. *Temurah* means permutation; the 'oh' on the end meaning 'His'. Thus is resolved this otherwise highly complex and confusing Hebrew sentence which yields the magical name ARARITA.

A very interesting example of this exegetical process is to be found in *The Golden Dawn*, Vol. I, p. 166, probably contributed by S.L. MacGregor Mathers:

Here is a method of writing Hebrew words by the Yetziratic attribution of the alphabet, whence results some curious hieroglyphic symbolism. Thus Tetragrammaton will be written Virgo, Aries, Taurus, Aries. *Eheieh*, by Air, Aires, Virgo, Aries. From *Yeheshuah*, the Qabalistic mode of spelling Jesus, which is simply the Tetragrammaton with the letter *Shin* placed therein, we obtain a very peculiar combination – Virgo, Aries, Fire, Taurus, Aries. Virgo born of a Virgin, Aries the Sacrificial Lamb, Fire the Fire of the Holy Spirit, Taurus the Ox of the Earth in whose Manger He was laid, and lastly Aries the flocks of sheep whose Herdsmen came to worship Him. *Elohim* yields Air, Libra, Aries, Virgo, Water – the Firmament, the Balanced Forces, the Fire of the Spirit (for Aries is a fiery sign) operating in the Zodiac, the Fire Goddess, and the Waters of Creation.

A much longer and more complex demonstration of Qabalistic methods of elucidation, which elaborate at greater length these simpler techniques, is to be found in the following example. Though I have tried to render this demonstration as simple as I can, it still needs to be followed with some care and attention.

I.N.R.I.

Let us take as a start, an old application of Qabalistic principles – the English letters I.N.R.I. They are, of course, the initials of a Latin phrase once placed by the Romans at the head of the Cross representing the phrase 'Jesus of Nazareth, King of the Jews'. Several other theological meanings to these letters have been given at different periods in history by various groups of people and scholars.

For example, the mediaeval alchemists suggested that I.N.R.I. meant 'Igne Natura Renovatur Integra' – the whole of Nature is renewed by fire.

Another example of about the same period elaborated the four letters to 'Igne Nitrum Raris Invenitum', translated as 'shining (or glittering) is rarely found in fire.'

The Jesuits in their day interpreted it as 'Justum Necare Regis Impius': 'It is just to kill an impious king.'

J.S.M. Ward in his book *Freemasonry and the Ancient Gods* gives another example:

I	*Yam* =	Water
N	*Nour* =	Fire
R	*Ruach* =	Air
I	*Yebeshah* =	Earth

Thus the four letters are Hebrew initials of the four ancient elements.

In the nineteenth century, when the Hermetic Order of the Golden Dawn came to be formed, these letters were picked up and integrated into the complex structure of the Order's symbolism. It was used as the keyword to one of its ritual grades, that of the Adeptus Minor. To follow the interpretation used by the Order we need only the most superficial knowledge of the attributions given in the *Sepher Yetzirah*, the Tarot pack of cards, a smattering of Gnosticism and astrology. The first gesture is to convert the four letters into their Hebrew equivalents and then to their direct Yetziratic attributions, as follows:

I	=	*Yod*	=	Virgo	=	♍
N	=	*Nun*	=	Scorpio	=	♏
R	=	*Resh*	=	Sun	=	☉
I	=	*Yod*	=	Virgo	=	♍

The final 'I', being repetitious, is dropped, only to be picked up again in a later place in order to extend the significance of the meanings derived from the analysis.

This breakdown, though it does not get us very far, is nonetheless highly suggestive. Elementary astrology will extend the meaning a little. Virgo represents the virginal sign of nature itself. Scorpio is the sign of death and transformation; sex is involved here as well. Sol, the sun, is the source of light and life to all on earth; it is the centre of our solar system. All the so-called resurrection gods are known to be connected with the sun. The sun was thought to die every winter when vegetation perished and the earth became cold and barren. Every spring, when the sun returned, green life was restored to the earth.

Then we could look at *Liber 777*, which codified most of the basic knowledge material of the Golden Dawn and added more as it was gradually acquired by its author, Aleister Crowley. In one of the columns of this book entitled 'Egyptian Gods' we find the following which we can add to the data already obtained.

Virgo = Isis – who was Nature, the Mother of all things.

Scorpio = Apophis – death, the destroyer.

Sol = Osiris – slain and risen, the Egyptian resurrection and vegetative God.

Here we begin to get a definite sequence of ideas that proves somewhat meaningful. The simplicity of a natural state of affairs in, shall we say, the Garden of Eden (representing the springtime of mankind) is shattered by the intrusion of the knowledge of Good and Evil, sexual perception. This is due to the intervention of the destroyer Apophis, or Lucifer the Lightbearer, who changed all things – by illuminating all things. Thus the Fall, as well as the fall of the year. This is succeeded by the advent of Osiris the resurrection God who stated 'This is my body, which I destroy in order that it may be renewed.' He is the symbolic prototype of the perfected Solar Man, who suffered through earthly experience, was glorified by trial, was betrayed and killed, and then rose again to renew all things.

The final analysis of the keyword sums up the formula with the initials of *I*sis, *A*pophis, *O*siris = IAO, the supreme God of the Gnostics (IAO is pronounced ee-ah-oh).

Since the sun is the giver of life and light, the formula must refer to light as the redeemer. The Order of the Golden Dawn was predicated on the age-old process of bringing light to the natural man. In other words, it taught psycho-spiritual techniques leading to illumination, to enlightenment. In this connection, one should always remember those beautiful versicles about the light in the opening chapter of the Gospel according to St John.

In the very first or Neophyte Ritual of the Golden Dawn, the candidate is startled to hear the strangely-worded invocation 'Khabs Am Pehkt. Konx om Pax. Light in Extension.' In other words, 'May you too receive the benediction of the light, and undergo the mystical experience, the goal of all our work.'

'The enlightenment by a ray of the divine light which transforms the psychic nature of man may be an article of faith,' says Hans Jonas in his excellent book *The Gnostic Religion*, 'but it may also be an experience ... Annihilation and deification of the person are fused in the spiritual ecstasis which purports to experience the immediate presence of the acosmic essence.'

> In the gnostic context, this transfiguring face-to-face experience is *gnosis* in the most exalted and at the same time the most paradoxical sense of the term, since it is knowledge of the unknowable ... The mystical *gnosis theôu* – direct beholding of the divine reality – is itself an earnest of the consummation to come. It is transcendence become immanent; and although prepared for by human acts of self-modification which induce the proper disposition, the event itself is one of divine activity and grace. It is thus as much a 'being known' by God as a 'knowing' Him, and in this ultimate mutuality the 'gnosis' is beyond the terms of 'knowledge' properly speaking.

Since this is the basic theme recurrent through all the Golden Dawn rituals and teaching, we would expect to find it repeated and expanded in the analysis of the keyword of the Adeptus Minor grade. And of course it is there, clearly defined.

The word light is translated into LVX, the Latin word for light. A series of physical mimes or gestures are made by the officiants to represent the descent of this light, as well as to summarize the symbolism of the previous findings.

So one Adept or officiant raises his right arm directly in the air above him, while extending his left arm straight outwards (as though to make a left turn when driving a car). This forms by shape the letter L.

A second Adept raises his arms as though in supplication above his head – the letter V.

The third Adept extends his arms outwards forming a cross.

All together finally cross their arms on their chests, forming the letter X.

(A single person may of course perform the identical gestures.)

In any event, the letters form LVX which is now interpreted as the Light of the Cross. It is so interpreted because the letters INRI were initially found on the Crucifix, and because LVX means light. Finally the letters LVX themselves are portions of one type or another of the Cross:

A process of repetition is followed in order to synthesize all these variegated ideas and gestures, and to add one more mime to replace the second 'I' that was eliminated for being repetitious.

As the L sign is being made, the Adept says: 'The Sign of the Mourning of Isis'. This expresses the sorrow of Isis on learning that Osiris had been slain by Set or Apophis.

As the V sign is made, the Adept says, 'The Sign of Apophis and Typhon'. These are the other names for Set, the brother and murderer of Osiris, whose body was so mutilated that only the phallus could be found by Isis who had searched all over creation for him.

As the Adept spreads his arms outward to the side forming actively the Cross, he says, 'The Sign of Osiris Slain'.

Then, crossing one arm over the other on the chest, he adds: 'And risen. Isis, Apophis, Osiris, IAO'.

Thus what started out to be a simple abbreviation of a traditional Latin sentence on the Cross above the head of Christ, has now evolved by a Qabalistic process of exegesis into a complex series of evocative ideas and symbolic gestures which extend tremendously the root idea. And by knowing these ideas, the gestures may be used practically to aspire to the illumination it suggests. This is the essential value of the sacramental actions.

The Rosicrucian equivalent of this formula is found in the *Fama Fraternitatis*, one of the original three classical Rosicrucian documents: 'Ex Deo Nascimur. In Jesu Morimur. Per spiritus sanctus reviviscimus.': 'From God are we born. In Christ we die. We are revived by the Holy Spirit.'

Nor is this all. If we take LVX as symbols of, Roman numerals, we have 65. This number, therefore, attains the symbolic equivalent of light, gnosis and illumination.

The Adeptus Minor obligation imposed on the candidate during the ritual initiation obligates him to aspire and work and practise so that by enlightenment he may one day 'become more than human'. This is the Qabalistic philosophy summarized in the statement that the Adept seeks to unite himself to his higher soul or his higher self, symbolized again in the Hebrew word *Adonai*. All the above notions therefore are synthesized in this word *Adonai*, literally translated 'My lord'. Its Hebrew letters are:

Aleph		*Daleth*		*Nun*		*Yod*		
1	+	4	+	50	+	10	=	65

This number is also that of LVX, light. Qabalistically, the process enables us to perceive a necessary connection between *Adonai* and the light – their identity.

Symbolism of the Heart and the Serpent

In 1907, when Aleister Crowley received some of his most meaningful illuminations after a decade of hard magical work and spiritual discipline, he wrote an inspirational book which he called *Liber LXV*, which we have seen is 65. Its sub-title was 'The Book of the Heart girt with a Serpent'. This latter phrase was extrapolated from the last section of an old ritual found in some scholarly texts entitled 'The Bornless Ritual'. Its last paragraph reads:

> I am He, the Bornless (or eternal) Spirit
> Having Sight in the feet, strong and the Immortal Fire.
> I am He, the Truth!
> I am He who hate that evil should be wrought in the world!
> I am He that lighteneth and thundereth!
> I am He from whom is the shower of the Life of Earth!
> I am He whose mouth ever flameth!
> I am He, the Grace of the World!
> *The Heart girt with a serpent is my name.*

It is the above underlined phrase which Crowley appropriated as the title of his illuminated book to bear witness to *Adonai*.

What of the symbols of the heart and the serpent? What meaning have they?

The heart has clear reference to the emotional life, to the inner core of man, to 'the heart of the matter', as we would colloquially say. And of the many titles given to Christ, one of them, 'The Sacred Heart', represents his passion, his sacrifice, and his redemptive love of mankind.

The serpent is an even more ancient and sophisticated symbol. It not only represents the abuse of the sexual force that corrupted and precipitated the Fall and expulsion from Eden, but also the transmuted and sublimated libido. Known as the *kundalini*, it is trained to arise out of the dark pelvic area, to course up the spine to form the golden aureole around the head of the saint or the fully enlightened adept.

> I am the Heart; and the Snake is entwined
> About the invisible core of the mind.
> Rise, O my snake! It is now the hour
> Of the hooded and holy ineffable flower.

Rise, O my snake, into brilliance of bloom
On the corpse of Osiris afloat in the tomb!
O heart of my mother, my sister, mine own,
Thou art given to Nile, to the terror Typhon!
Ah me! but the glory of ravening storm
Enswathes thee and wraps thee in frenzy of form.
Be still, O my soul! that the spell may dissolve
As the wands are upraised, and the aeons revolve.
Behold! in my beauty how joyous Thou art,
O Snake that caresses the crown of mine heart!
Behold! We are one, and the tempest of years
Goes down to the dusk, and the Beetle appears.
O Beetle! the drone of Thy dolorous note
Be ever the trance of this tremulous throat!
I await the awakening! The summons on high,
From the Lord Adonai, from the Lord Adonai!

Regarding *Adonai*, the title given to the Holy Guardian Angel, we could pay some little attention to the very last verse in *Liber LXV* as having some further bearing on this task of exegesis. It says: 'And my lord Adonai is about me on all sides, like a thunderbolt, like a pylon, like a serpent, and like a phallus, and in the midst thereof he is like the woman that jetteth out the milk of the stars from her paps, yea, the milk of the stars from her paps.'

It may sound ludicrous perhaps and most obscure until we commence the task of elucidation using our basic Qabalistic tools.

A = *Aleph* = thunderbolt by shape and by attribution.
D = *Daleth* = literally a gate; thus a pylon.
N = *Nun* = literally a fish, attributed to Scorpio, one of whose triune meanings is the serpent.
I = *Yod* = finger of the hand; even in Freudian terms it is the symbol of the phallus.

Thus, the first part of the term simply explicates and emphasizes that the Lord Adonai surrounds one on all sides. One is altogether enclosed within his divinity. The woman who jetteth forth the milk of the stars from her breasts is of course Nuit, the Lady of the Starry Heavens, the Egyptian symbol of Infinite Space, within which the nebulae appear, and thus cognate with *Ain Soph*. The *Adonai* is a spiritual centre within the boundlessness of the Infinite Light, and in a sense symbolized the infinite God to the finite natural man.

Further about the serpent: for example, Hans Jonas in his authoritative text *The Gnostic Religion*, had this to say:

More than one gnostic sect derived its name from the cult of the *serpent* ('Ophites' from the Greek *ophis*: 'Naasenes' from the Hebrew *nahas* – the group as a whole being termed 'ophitic') and this position of the serpent is based on a bold allegorizing of the biblical text ... The Peratae, sweepingly consistent, did not even shrink from regarding the historical Jesus as a particular incarnation of the 'general serpent', i.e., the serpent from Paradise understood as a principle ... By Mani's time (third century) the gnostic interpretation of the Paradise story and Jesus' connection with it had become so firmly established that he could simply put Jesus in the place of the serpent with no mention of the latter.

There are some interesting possibilities here, for in Hebrew there is a word *nachosh*, a serpent. Analysing the word as before, we obtain:

N   = *Nun* = Scorpio = Serpent = 50
Ch = *Cheth* = Cancer = The Chariot in Tarot = 8
Sh = *Shin* = Fire = The Holy Spirit = 300.

The total enumeration is 358.
Now we must consult *Sepher Sephiroth* once more. There we find under the same number another Hebrew word *Meschiach*, translated as the Messiah, the anointed one:

M   = *Mem* = Water = The Hanged Man in Tarot = 40
Sh = *Shin* = Fire = The Holy Spirit = 300
Y   = *Yod* = Virgo = The Hermit in Tarot = 10
CH = *Cheth* = Cancer = The Chariot in Tarot = 8.

This, too, adds up to 358. Inferentially, therefore, we must deduce that the serpent and the Messiah have much in common. By means of the serpent power, the interior transforming fire of the spirit, the Adept becomes transformed into a Messiah or a Redeemer to his own inner world at the very least, if not in some occult manner to mankind as a whole. Each man who gains freedom thereby renders freedom a greater possibility to other men.
Now look at the sequence of ideas in each of these two words. The serpent transforms the Adept into a '*Mercabah* (chariot) - rider' towards his mystical home in the Infinite Light – that is to say, it is the powerful agent involved in his illumination. The second word yields analogous material. By sacrifice of all extraneous factors, the Holy Spirit or the Guardian Angel, acting as the hermit or silent illuminator of mankind, ascends Ezekiel's chariot and moves heavenward.

IAO

Then there is the Gnostic name of God – IAO. It is one of those archaic names of which the so-called *Chaldean Oracles* says: 'Change not the barbarous names of evocation for they have a power ineffable in the sacred rites.' Well may we ask, what kind of power does this name have? This question may be answered by transliterating the name into Hebrew. From there, its Yetziratic attributions will provide a degree of enlightenment. There are two ways of doing this; both are interesting.

$$I = Yod = \text{Virgo} = 10$$
$$A = Aleph = \text{Air} = 1 \quad\Big\} = 17$$
$$O = Vau = \text{Taurus} = 6$$

Seventeen represents the number of squares in the swastika or Fylfot Cross. By shape it represents *Aleph*, the thunderbolt. And *Aleph* is the first letter of the alphabet, and is 1.

The second way provides a slightly different result:

$$I = Yod = \text{Virgo} = 10$$
$$A = Aleph = \text{Air} = 1 \quad\Big\} = 81$$
$$O = Ayin = \text{Capricorn} = 70$$

81 is a mystic number of the moon. Luna is attributed to *Yesod*, the Foundation. Its number is 9. The magical square of Luna is 9 x 9, giving 81 squares. This does not fit into our discussion in the least, so the previous method is more appropriate.

If the numerical value of IAO, then, is 17, referred to *Aleph* and so the thunderbolt, by the symbolism described above, we have a much clearer idea of the divine power involved. It is that of the Father of all the Gods wielding the thunderbolt (the Scandinavian swastika or the Tibetan *dorje*) to further his intent of creation. Furthermore, notice that we have *Aleph*, the thunderbolt acting in the divine Air, sandwiched between two earthy signs, Virgo and Taurus, whirling their substance into the appropriate function of creation.

What a long way we have gone from 'Jesus of Nazareth, King of the Jews'. And if our Qabalistic methods will enable us to gain this much insight from merely four letters, it can be left to the student to gather to what lengths we can go to become enlightened on the basis of other words and other ideas. They will show how vast are the possibilities involved in but a single word or sentence. The English translation of the *Zohar* presents innumerable examples of exegesis of many simple biblical notions. Before you know where you are you have been swept away on an exciting wave of spiritual adventure that can only end with the melting of the soul in its divine source.

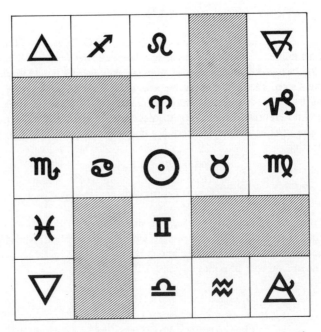

The Swastika (considered as a Fylfot Cross of seventeen squares).

To conclude this essay, I am going to select one or two more examples, which are fairly complex in substance and import, in order to demonstrate how some of these Qabalistic modes of exegesis work. This particular example is from *The Vision and The Voice, Liber 418*, second part of the Fourteenth Aethyr (Equinox V, Supplement):

> The blackness gathers about, so thick, so clinging, so penetrating, so oppressive, that all the other darkness that I have ever conceived would be like bright light beside it.
>
> His voice comes in a whisper: O thou that art master of the fifty gates of Understanding, is not my mother a black woman? O thou that art master of the Pentagram, is not the egg of spirit a black egg? Here abideth terror, and the blind ache of the Soul, and lo! even I, who am the sole light, a spark shut up, stand in the sign of Apophis and Typhon.
>
> I am the snake that devoureth the spirit of man with the lust of light. I am the sightless storm in the night that wrappeth the world about with desolation. Chaos is my name, and thick darkness. Know thou that the darkness of the earth is ruddy, and the darkness of the air is grey, but the darkness of the soul is utter blackness.

The egg of the spirit is a basilisk egg, and the gates of the understanding are fifty, that is the sign of the Scorpion. The pillars about the neophyte are crowned with flame, and the vault of the Adepts is lighted by the Rose. And in the abyss is the eye of the hawk. But upon the great sea shall the Master of the Temple find neither star nor moon."

Exegetical Analysis

This whole speech is one of crossing the abyss and the visionary entry into the *Sephirah* of *Binah*, the third emanation on The Tree of Life. It is attributed to the Great Sea, from which all life has emerged, to the planet Saturn which is the planet of death as well as of stability. It is further attributed to *Aimah Elohim*, the mother of the Gods and to Isis as well, the goddess of Nature, to Babalon who is the goddess representing Shakti, which is the universal creative energy and joy, amongst many other meanings. With these basic clues, much of what is cryptically stated in the vision becomes relatively clear.

Since the vision opens with blackness, this becomes a fundamental declaration that the seer is on the right track. All the symbols are harmonious, and the association pathways are not cluttered with inappropriate symbols.

Binah is translated as 'understanding'. And since attributed to Saturn and death, a related symbol would be Scorpio which is attributed to the Tarot card 'Death', usually meaning involuntary change, transformation, sublimation. The *Sepher Yetzirah* letter relative to Scorpio is *Nun*, which means a fish, and its number is 50. These are the gates of understanding, fifty in number, all links in a long but valid chain of associations. Scorpio is also the basilisk. Saturn is black, the colour of mourning. Since Isis, the great Mother, is attributed to this sphere, we have the statement, 'Is not my mother a black woman?' And, as we have learned earlier, the sign of Apophis and Typhon is the sign of destruction.

To each of the five points of the Pentagram is attributed one of the five elements. The five-pointed signet star is in the shape of the perfected man who has developed all phases of his personality represented by the elements. Each of the latter has its own symbols. In the Eastern system, spirit, the quintessence or *Akasa*, is represented by an upstanding black egg.

Binah is also represented by the correspondence of night, the darkest blackest kind of night which Crowley at one time poetically represented by the City of the Pyramids under the N.O.X. or Night of Pan, and at times by the name of a former lady friend Leila, which he promptly transliterated into Hebrew – thus *Laylah*, meaning Night. In this way he transformed a personal relationship into a symbol of a high spiritual experience. These attributions are all referred to *Binah* and *Shekinah* – the divine Presence of the immanence of God, and to Chaos, the realm of the unformed and uncreated.

The vision as a whole, therefore, relates to *Binah* and Scorpio, to death and rebirth, to the transformation of the ego-ridden man into NEMO, 'no man', because by dying to self, he has become identified with the Holy Spirit of all that lives, the Self.

The Fama Fraternitatis

One of the old Rosicrucian classics previously mentioned is the *Fama Fraternitatis*. It was first published at Cassel, Germany, and of course circulated freely amongst mystics, alchemists and occultists of the time in Europe. An unabridged version of the *Fama*, together with some of the other Rosicrucian classics, is to be found in an excellent book entitled *Rosicrucian Fundamentals* (New York, 1923) by Khei X° (the late George Winslow Plummer) of the Societas Rosicruciana in America. In Arthur Edward Waite's book *The Brotherhood of the Rosy Cross* (University Press, New York, *circa* 1963) an edited version is to be found.

The *Fama* purports to give the history of the founder of the Rosicrucian Order, one Brother C.R.C. or Christian Rosencreutz, said to have been born in 1378. His education and travels are delineated at some length. Parts of this dramatic history were extrapolated for inclusion into the Adeptus Minor ritual of the Golden Dawn. A great deal of Qabalistic exegesis has been undertaken on the basis of this history by various members of the Order at different times. Perhaps the most readily accessible is *The True and Invisible Rosicrucian Order* written by Paul Foster Case. This latter book goes into such extraordinary detail and analysis of the minutiae of the *Fama* and other early Rosicrucian documents that perhaps the beginner is likely to be overwhelmed by the great wealth and skill of exposition demonstrated by the author. The more advanced student will see in it a useful source book upon which he can build, by his own ever-expanding knowledge of the methods depicted here and by his own meditations.

I select one or two names from the *Fama* to indicate how they can be elucidated by means of the Qabalah of number and symbol. For example, the story narrates that C.R.C. made a bargain with the Arabians to take him to Damcar. Some of the early commentators have suggested that this was Damascus. But since the legend is symbolic these names need to be interpreted symbolically.

If we transliterate Damcar into Hebrew, following our previous rules, we have two words: *dam* (*Daleth* and *Mem*), which means blood, and *car* (*Caph* and *Resh*), a word meaning lamb. Our name place, then, becomes transformed into a symbol of the 'Blood of the Lamb'. Of course the Rosicrucians were Christians, and Christians of the Reformation; but being mystics they interpreted the traditional Christian body of knowledge in a symbolic manner. So 'The blood of the Lamb which taketh away the sins of the world' of necessity was taken symbolically by them.

The Lamb is *Agni* in the Hindu Scriptures, symbol of the sacrificial fire, and of course in the West it is Christ. As indicated in the essay on meditation (page 85), it is hypothesized that meditation accompanied by other occult work succeeds in altering the chemistry of the blood, which in turn changes the normal function of the cerebral cortex. The result of this is that, with the cessation of cerebral or cortical activity, illumination can occur. That is to say, the ego is eclipsed and the Adept for the time being becomes, or realizes, he is a vehicle for the divine spirit, the Lamb of God.

The temple at Damcar where C.R.C. was taken by the Arabs, who at that time were the repositors of the ancient knowledge, is thus the Adept himself, his own organism. For are we not told that the body is the Temple of the Holy Ghost? Thus it is implied that the Arabs who took him to Damcar initiated him into some of the secrets of practical occultism so that he became a vehicle for the transmission of the forces of the higher spiritual planes.

But let us look at the Gematria of these two words:

$$Dam = \quad Daleth + Mem \quad \text{and} \quad Car = \quad Caph + Resh$$
$$4 \quad + \quad 40 = 44 \qquad\qquad 20 + 200 \quad = 220$$

We can take the words separately and then together. For example, *dam* (44) which means blood, equates with words for a ram *(telah)* and flame *(lehat)* and sorrow *(agam)*. These words are taken from *Sephir Sephiroth*, which has several words tabulated under specific numbers. Some little meditation by the student will enable him to integrate these words together under the aegis of the primary exegetical meaning of 'The Blood of the Lamb'.

The word *car* (220), meaning lamb, equates with *Baher* (the Elect) as well as one of the Old Testament words *nephilim* (meaning giants). The student should not experience much difficulty in relating these words with our basic term.

On the other hand, if we take Damcar with the number 264, we find in *Sepher Sephiroth* words like *chekokim*, meaning hollows or cavities, and *rehòtim* meaning channels, troughs, or pipes. These two latter words were originally used in connection with the ten *Sephiroth* of The Tree of Life, implying that they were cavities or channels through which flowed *Mezla*, the divine life and spirit.

One final manipulation reveals a little bit more. $2+6+4 = 12$. This number was dealt with on an earlier page in connection with the path of Gimel, the High Priestess of the Tarot. All of these words and numbers and symbols are descriptive of Damcar, and meditation will enlarge the concept still further.

Conclusion

These are some of the approaches taken by the Qabalists of many schools, ancient and modern, Hebrew and Christian, orthodox as well as what G.S. Scholem has mistakenly called nihilistic mysticism. Some of these methods may appear to be strained and arbitrary. Perhaps they are. At the same time, however, should they elicit even a shred of meaning from otherwise obscure texts, and illuminate the darkness of sterile scriptures that some feel may be important, then we can take the simple point of view that they have served a useful purpose.

5. THE ART OF TRUE HEALING

1.

Within every man and woman is a force which directs and controls the entire course of life. Properly used, it can heal every affliction and ailment to which mankind is heir. Every single religion affirms this fact. All forms of mental or spiritual healing, no matter under what name they travel, promise the same thing. Even psychoanalysis employs this power, though indirectly, using the now popular word *libido*. For the critical insight and understanding which it brings to bear upon the psyche releases tensions of various kinds, and through this release the healing power latent within and natural to the human system operates more freely. Each of these systems undertakes to teach its devotees technical methods of thinking or contemplation or prayer such as will, according to the *a priori* terms of their own philosophies, renew their bodies and transform their whole environment.

None or few of them, however, actually fulfil in a complete way the high promise made at the outset. There seems but little understanding of the practical means whereby the spiritual forces underlying the universe and permeating the entire nature of man may be utilized and directed towards the creation of a new heaven and a new earth. Naturally, without universal co-operation, such an ideal is impossible for all mankind. Nevertheless, each one for himself may commence the task of reconstruction.

The crucial question, then, is how are we to become aware of this force? What are its nature and properties? What is the mechanism whereby we can use it?

Untapped Currents

As I have said before, different systems have evolved widely differing processes, by which the student might divine the presence of such a power. Meditation, prayer, invocation, emotional exaltation, and demands made at random upon the universe or the Universal Mind, have been a few of such methods. In the last resort, if we ignore petty details of a trivial nature, all have this in common. By turning the fiery penetrating power of the mind inwards upon itself, and exalting the emotional system to a certain pitch, we may become aware of previously unsuspected currents of force. Currents, moreover, almost electric in their interior sensation, healing and integrating in their effect.

It is the willed use of such a force that is capable of bringing health to body and mind. When directed it acts magnet-like. By this I mean that it attracts to whomsoever employs these methods just those necessities of life, material or spiritual, that he urgently requires or which are needed for his further evolution.

Fundamentally, the underlying idea of the mental healing systems is this. In the ambient atmosphere surrounding us and pervading the structure of each minute body cell is a spiritual force. This force is omnipresent and infinite. It is present in the most infinitesimal object as it is in the most proportion-staggering nebula or island universe. It is this force which is life itself. Nothing in the vast expanse of space is dead. Everything pulsates with vibrant life. Even the ultra-microscopic particles of the atom are alive; in fact the electron is a crystallization of its electric power.

This life force being infinite it follows that man must be saturated – permeated through and through with spiritual force. It constitutes his higher self, it is his link with godhead, it is God in man. Every molecule in his physical system must be soaked with its dynamic energy. Each cell in the body contains it in its plenitude. Thus we are brought face to face with the enormous problem underlying all disease, the enigmatical problem of nervous depletion.

What is Fatigue?

How *can* there be depletion if vitality and cosmic currents of force daily pour through man, simply saturating his mind and body with its power? Primarily, it is because he offers so much resistance to its flow through him that he becomes tired and ill, the conflict finally culminating in death. How is puny man able to defy the universe? Nay more, offer resistance and opposition to the very force which underlies, and continually evolves in, the universe? The complacency and confusion of his mental outlook, the moral cowardice by which he was reared, and his false perception of the nature of life – these are the causes of resistance to the inward flow of the spirit. That this is unconscious is no logical obstacle to the force of this argument, as all the depth psychologies have demonstrated. What man is really aware of all the involuntary processes going on within him? Who is conscious of the intricate mechanism of his mental processes, of that by which his food is assimilated and digested, of the circulation of his blood, of the arterial distribution of nourishment to every bodily organ? All these are purely involuntary processes: to a large degree so are his resistances to life. Man has surrounded himself with a crystallized shell of prejudices and ill-conceived fantasies, an armour which affords no entrance to the light of life without.

What wonder he ails? What wonder he is so ill and impotent, helpless and poor? Why should there be surprise that the average individual is so unable adequately to deal with life?

The First Two Steps to Health

The first step towards freedom and health is a conscious realization of the vast spiritual reservoir in which we live and move and have our being. Repeated intellectual effort to make this part and parcel of one's mental outlook upon life automatically breaks down or dissolves something of the hard inflexible shell of the mind. And then life and spirit pour abundantly. Health spontaneously arises, and a new life begins as the point of view undergoes this radical change. Moreover, it would appear that the environment attracts just those people who can help in various ways, and precisely those amenities of life that had been longed for.

The second step lies in a slightly different direction. Regulated breathing – quite a simple process. Its necessity follows from the following postulate. If life is all about one, all-penetrating and all-pervasive, what more reasonable than that the very air we breathe from one moment to another should be highly charged with vitality? Our breathing processes we therefore regulate accordingly. We contemplate that life is the active principle in the atmosphere. During the practice of this rhythmical breathing at fixed periods of the day, there should be no strenuous forcing of the mind, no overtaxing of the will. We let the breath flow in while mentally counting very slowly ... one, two, three, four. Then we exhale counting the same beat. It is fundamental and important that the initial rhythm, whether it be a four or a ten beat count or any other convenient one, should be maintained. For it is the very rhythm itself which is responsible for the easy absorption of vitality from without, and the acceleration of the divine power within.

Rhythm

Immutable rhythm is everywhere manifest in the universe. It is a living process whose parts move and are governed in accordance with the cyclic laws. Look at the sun, the stars, and the planets. All move with comparable grace, with a rhythm in their inexorable times. It is only mankind that has wandered, in its ignorance and self-complacency, far from the divine cycles of things. We have interfered with the rhythmic process inherent in nature. And how sadly have we paid for it!

Therefore, in attempting to attune ourselves once more to the intelligent spiritual power functioning through nature's mechanism, we attempt, not blindly to copy, but intelligently to adopt her methods. Make, therefore, the breathing rhythmical at certain fixed times of the day, when there is little likelihood of disturbance. Cultivate above all the art of relaxation. Learn to address each tensed muscle from toe to head as you lie flat on your back in bed. Tell it deliberately to loosen its tension and cease from its unconscious contracture. Think of the blood in response to your command flowing copiously to each organ, carrying life and nourishment everywhere, producing a state of glowing, radiant health. Only after these preliminary processes have been accomplished should you begin your rhythmic breathing, slowly and without haste. Gradually, as the mind accustoms itself to the idea, the lungs will take up the rhythm spontaneously. In a few minutes it will have become automatic. The whole process then becomes extremely simple and pleasurable.

It would be impossible to overestimate its importance or efficacy. As the lungs take up the rhythm, automatically inhaling and exhaling to a measured beat, so do they communicate it and gradually extend it to all the surrounding cells and tissue – just as a stone thrown into a pool sends out widely expanding ripples and concentric circles of motion. In a few minutes the whole body is vibrating in unison with their movement. Every cell seems to vibrate sympathetically. And very soon, the whole organism comes to feel as if it were an inexhaustible storage battery of power. The sensation – and it *must* be a sensation – is unmistakable.

Simple as it is, the exercise is not to be despised. It is upon the mastery of this very easy technique that the rest of this system stands. Master it first. Make sure that you can completely relax and then produce the rhythmic breath in a few seconds.

Mental and Spiritual Centres

I now approach an idea fundamental and highly significant. It is the inability to realize or thoroughly to have grasped its importance which really underlies the frequently observed failure of many mental culture and spiritual healing systems. Just as in the physical body are specialized organs for the performance of specialized functions, so in the mental and spiritual nature exist corresponding centres and organs. Exactly as the teeth, the stomach, liver and intestines are so many mechanisms evolved and devised by nature for the digestion and assimilation of food, so are there similar centres in the other constituents of man's nature.

The mouth receives food. Digestion occurs in the stomach and small intestines. Likewise there is an apparatus for rejecting waste effete products. In the psychic nature also are focal centres for the absorption of spiritual power from the universe without. Others render its distribution and circulation possible. The dynamic energy and power entering man from without is not uniform or alike in vibratory rate. It may be of too high a voltage, so to say, readily to be endured by him. Within, therefore, is a certain psychic apparatus whereby indiscriminate cosmic currents of energy may be assimilated and digested, their voltage thus becoming stepped down or adjusted to the human level. The process of becoming aware of this psychic apparatus, and using the energy it generates, is an integral part of this healing system.

It is my contention that prayer and contemplative methods unconsciously employ these inner centres. Hence we would be wiser and far more efficient deliberately to employ for our own ends this spiritual power and the centres it flows through. Let us call these latter, for the moment, psycho-spiritual organs, of which there are five major ones. Since name them we must, inasmuch as the human mind loves to classify and tabulate things, let me give them the most non-committal and non-compromising titles imaginable so that no system of prejudice may be erected theron. For convenience's sake, the first we may name Spirit, the second Air, the succeeding ones being called Fire, Water and Earth.

To illustrate the concept, I reproduce here a simple diagram. It shows the position and location of the centres. Not for one moment do I wish to be understood as stating that these centres are physical in nature and position (though there may be glandular parallelisms). They exist in a subtler spiritual or psychic part of man's nature. We may even consider them, not as realities themselves, but as symbols of realities, great, redeeming and saving symbols. Under certain conditions we may become aware of them in very much the same way as we may become aware of different organs in our physical bodies. We often speak of reason as being situated in the head, referring emotion to the heart and instinct to the belly. Similarly, there exists a natural correspondence between these centres and various parts of the body.

Thought, Colour and Sound

It is axiomatic to this system that there are three principal engines or means whereby we may become aware of these centres to awaken them from their dormant state so that they may function properly within. Thought, colour, and sound are the three means. The mind

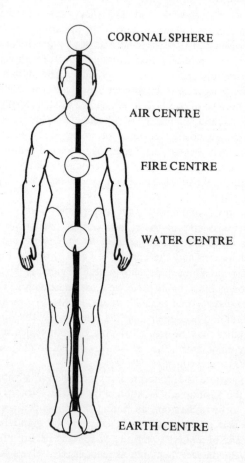

CORONAL SPHERE

AIR CENTRE

FIRE CENTRE

WATER CENTRE

EARTH CENTRE

The Five Centres.

must concentrate itself on the assumed position of these centres one by one. Then certain names which are to be considered as vibratory rates must be intoned and vibrated. Finally, each centre is to be visualized as having a particular colour and shape. The combination of these three agencies gradually awakens the centres from their latency. Slowly they become stimulated into functioning each according to its own nature, pouring forth a stream of highly spiritualized energy and power into the body and mind. When, utlimately, their operation becomes habitual and stabilized, the spiritual power they generate may be directed by will to heal various ailments and diseases both of a psychological and physical nature. It can also be communicated by a mere laying on of hands to another person. Simply by thinking fixedly and with intent, the energy, moreover, can be communicated from mind to mind telepathically or transmitted through space to another person miles away – objects in space affording no interruption or obstacle to its passage.

The Coronal Sphere

First of all, the position of the centres, as shown in the diagram, must be memorized. They are to be stimulated into activity either while sitting upright or whilst lying down flat on the back in a perfectly relaxed state. The hands may be folded in the lap, or else, with fingers interlocked, be permitted to rest loosely below the solar plexus. Calmness of mind should be induced, and several minutes devoted to rhythmic breathing should result in the sensation of a gentle ripple playing over the diaphragm.

Then imagine above the coronal region of the head a ball or sphere of brilliant white light. Do not *force* the imagination to visualize the light sphere. To force would only result in the development of neuromuscular tension, and this would defeat our end. Let it be done quietly and easily. If the mind wanders, as indeed it will, wait a moment or two and gently lead it back. At the same time vibrate or intone the word *Eheieh*, pronounced as *Eh-huh-yeh*. After a few days of practice it will become quite easy to imagine the name vibrating above the head in the so-called Spirit centre. This is the indwelling or overshadowing divinity in each one of us, the basic spiritual self which we can all draw upon. *Eheieh* means literally I AM, and this centre represents the I AM consciousness within.

The effect of thus mentally directing the vibration is to awaken the centre to dynamic activity. When once it begins to vibrate and rotate, light and energy are felt to emanate downwards upon and into the personality. Enormous charges of spiritual power make their way into the brain, and the entire body feels suffused with vitality and life. Even the finger-tips and toes react to the awakening of the coronal sphere by a faint pricking sensation at first being felt. The name should be intoned during the first few weeks of practice in a moderately audible and sonorous tone of voice. As skill is acquired, then the vibration may be practised in silence, the name being imagined and mentally placed in the centre. If the mind tends to wander, the frequent repetition of the vibration will be found a great help to concentration.

The Air Centre

Having let the mind rest here for some five minutes, when it will be seen to glow and scintillate, imagine that it emits a white shaft downwards through the skull and brain, stopping at the throat. Here it expands to form a second ball of light, which should include a large part of the face, up to and including the eyebrows. If the larynx is conceived to be the centre of the sphere, then the distance from it to the cervical vertebrae at the back of the neck will be approximately the radius. Naturally this dimension will vary with different people. A similar technique should be pursued with this sphere, which we name the Air centre, as obtained with the previous one. It should be strongly and vividly formulated as a scintillating sphere of brilliant white light, shining and glowing from within. The name to be vibrated is *Jehovah Elohim* – pronounced as *Yuh-hoh-voh Eh-loh-heem.*

A word or two may not be amiss at this point with regard to the names. In reality they are names ascribed in various parts of the Old Testament to God. The variety and variation of these names are attributed to different divine functions. When acting in a certain manner, He is described by the biblical scribes by one name. When doing something else, another name more appropriate to His action is used. The system I am describing now has its roots in the Hebrew mystical tradition. Its ancient innovators were men of exalted religious aspirations and genius. It is only to be expected that a religious bias was projected by them into this scientific psychological system. But it must be explained that for our present-day purposes no religious connotation is implied by my use of these biblical divine names. Anyone may use them without subscribing in the least to the ancient religious views – whether he be a Jew, Christian, Hindu, Buddhist or atheist. It is a purely empirical system which is successful despite the scepticism or faith of the operator. We today may consider these sacred names in an entirely different and practical light. They are keynotes of different constituents of man's nature, doorways to so many levels of that part of the psyche of which normally we are unconscious. They are vibratory rates or symbolic signatures of the psychophysical centres we are describing. Their use as vibratory keynotes awakens into activity the centres with which their rate is in sympathy, conveying to our consciousness some recognition of the several levels of the unconscious spiritual side of our personalities. Hence the actual religious significance does not concern us. Nor their literal translation.

To refer back to the Air centre in the throat, let the vibratory sounds be intoned a number of times, until its existence is recognized and clearly felt as a definite sensory experience. There is no mistaking the sensation of its awakening. About the same length of time should be spent formulating it and the succeeding centres as was devoted to the contemplation of the coronal sphere. This period having elapsed, let it thrust downward from itself, with the aid of imagination, a shaft of light.

The Fire Centre

Descending to the region of the solar plexus, just beneath the sternum or breast-bone, the shaft expands once again to form a third sphere. This is the position of the Fire centre. The allocation of fire to this centre is particularly appropriate, for the heart is notoriously associated with the emotional nature, with love and the higher feelings. How often do we not speak of ardent passion, and the flame of love, and so forth? The diameter of this ambient cardiac sphere should be such as to extend from the front of the body to the back. Here vibrate the name *Jehovah Eloah ve-Daas*, pronounced as *Yuh-hoh-voh Eh-loh ve-Dah-ahs*. Take care that the intonation vibrates well within the formulated white sphere. If this is done, at once a radiation of warmth will be felt to emanate from the centre, gently stimulating all the parts and organs about it. Some students have complained that the above divine name is unduly long and difficult to pronounce. After some experimentation, I have substituted the gnostic name IAO for the Hebrew word. Both are attributed, qabalistically, to the *Sephirah* of *Tiphareth* on The Tree of Life, and so are equally valid. I have found it to be every bit as effective as the Hebrew name, and in my own practice of this meditation I have permanently substituted the one for the other.

IAO should be pronounced eee-(as in *key*) ah-oh, slowly and with vigour. In point of fact, it is simpler to vibrate this name than almost any other, and the vibration it produces is clear and strong.

Since the mind functions in and through the body, being co-extensive with it, the mental and emotional faculties likewise become stimulated by the dynamic flow of energy from the centres. The hard and fast barrier erected between consciousness and the unconscious, an armoured partition which impedes our free expression and hinders spiritual development, slowly becomes dissolved. As time goes on, and the practice continues, it may disappear completely and the personality gradually achieve integration and wholeness. Thus health spreads to every function of mind and body and happiness ensues as a permanent blessing.

The Water Centre

Continue the shaft downwards from the solar plexus to the pelvic region, the region of the generative organs. Here, too, a radiant sphere is to be visualized approximately of the same dimensions as the higher one. Here also is a name to be intoned so as to produce a rapid vibration in the cells and molecules of the tissue in that region. *Shaddai El Chai* is to be pronounced *Shah-di El Chi* (remember the *ch* is guttural as in 'loch'). The mind must be permitted to dwell on the imaginative formulation for some minutes, visualizing the sphere as of a white brilliance. And each time the mind wanders from such a brilliance, as at the beginning it is bound to do, let it gently be coaxed back by repeated and powerful vibrations of the name.

It may be feared that this practice could awaken or stimulate sexual feeling and emotion unnecessarily. In those in whom a sexual conflict is raging such an apprehension is just and legitimate. Actually, however, the fear is groundless. For the contemplation of the Water centre as a sphere of white light connected by a shaft to the higher and more spiritual centres acts rather in a more sedative way. And in point of fact sexual stimulation can be removed, not by ignorant and short-sighted repression, but by the circulation of such energies through the system by means of this practice. A thoroughgoing and far-reaching process of sublimation, alchemical almost in effect, may thus be instigated. This is not to be construed as legitimizing the avoidance of the sexual problem.

The Earth Centre

The final step is once more to visualize the shaft descending from the reproductive sphere, moving downwards through the thighs and legs until it strikes the feet. There it expands from a point approximately beneath the ankle, and forms a fifth sphere. We have named this one the Earth centre. Let the mind formulate here exactly as before a brilliant dazzling sphere of the same size as the others. Vibrate the name *Adonai ha-Aretz* as *Ah-doh-ni hah-Ah-retz*. Several minutes having been utilized in awakening this centre by fixed and steady thought and by repeated vibration of the name, pause for a short while.

Then try to visualize clearly the entire shaft of silvery light, studded as it were with five gorgeous diamonds of incomparable brilliance, stretching from the crown of the head to the soles of the feet. But a few minutes will suffice to give reality to this concept, bringing about a vivid realization of the powerful forces which, playing upon the personality, are eventually assimilated into the psychophysical system after their transformation and passage through the imaginative centres. The combination of rhythmic breathing with the willed visualization of the descent of power through the light shaft or Middle Pillar, as it is also called, produces by far the best results.

Colour Correspondences

As skill and familiarity are acquired in the formulation of the centres, an addition to the technique may be made. Earlier I remarked that colour was a very important consideration where this technique was concerned. Each centre has a different colour attribution, though it is wisest for a long period of time to refrain from using any other colour than white. To the Spirit or coronal centre the colour white is attributed. It is the colour of purity, spirit, divinity, and so on. It represents, not so much a human constituent, but a universal and cosmic principle overshadowing the whole of mankind. As we descend the shaft, however, the colours change. Lavender is attributed to the Air or throat centre, and it represents particularly the mental faculties – human consciousness as such.

To the Fire centre, red is an obvious association requiring no further comment. Blue is the colour referred to the Water centre; it is the colour of peace, calmness and tranquillity, concealing enormous strength and virility. In other words, its peace is the peace of strength and power rather than the inertia of mere weakness. Finally, the colour referred to the lowest centre of Earth is russet, the rich deep colour of the earth itself, the foundation upon which we rest.

From this very brief and concise summary it will be seen that each of these centres has a species of affinity or sympathy with a different spiritual constituent. One centre is peculiarly sympathetic to or is associated with the emotions and feelings, whilst another has definitely an intellectual bias. Hence, it follows logically, and experience demonstrates this fact, that their equilibrated activity and stimulation evokes a sympathetic reaction from every part of man's nature. And where disease manifesting in the body is directly due to some psychic maladjustment or infirmity, then the activity of the appropriate centre must be considered as affected somehow in a deleterious way. Its stimulation by sound, thought and colour, tends to stimulate the corresponding psychic principle and thus to disperse the maladjustment. Sooner or later a reaction is induced physically in the disappearance of the disease, and the consequent building up of new cells and tissue – the appearance of health itself.

2.

We approach a further and important stage in the development of the Middle Pillar technique. Having brought power and spiritual energy into the system by means of the psycho-spiritual centres, how best are we to use it? That is to say, use it in such a way that every single cell, every atom, and every organ becomes stimulated and vitalized by that dynamic stream?

To begin with, we throw the mind upwards to the coronal sphere again, imagining it to be in a state of vigorous activity. That is, it revolves rapidly, absorbing spiritual energy from space about it, transforming it in such a way that it becomes available for immediate use in any human activity. Imagine then that such transformed energy flows, stream-like, down the left side of the head, down the left side of the trunk and the left leg. While the current is descending the breath should slowly be exhaled to a convenient rhythm. With the slow inhalation of the breath, imagine that the vital current passes from the sole of the left foot to the right foot, and gradually ascends the right side of the body. In this way it returns to the source from which it issued, the coronal centre, the human source of all energy and vitality, a closed electrical circuit thus being established. Naturally this circulation is visualized as persisting within the body rather than as travelling around the periphery of the physical shape. It is, so to say, an interior psychic circulation rather than a purely physical one.

Stimulating Circulation

Let this circulation, once firmly established by the mind, flow evenly to the rhythm of the breath for some seconds so that the circuit has been traversed about half a dozen times — or even more, if you wish. Then repeat it in a slightly different direction. Visualize the vital flow as moving from the coronal centre above the head down the front of the face and body. After having turned backwards under the soles of the feet, it ascends at the back in a fairly wide belt of vibrating energy. This, likewise should accompany the inhalation and exhalation of breath, and should also be persisted in for at least six complete circuits.

The general effect of these two movements will be to establish in and about the physical form an ovoid shape of swiftly circulating substance and power. Since the spiritual energy dealt with by this technique is extremely dynamic and kinetic, it radiates in every direction, spreading outwards to an appreciable distance. It is this radiation which forms, colours and informs the ovoid sphere of sensation which is not conterminous with the shape or dimension of the physical frame. General perception and experience has it that the sphere of luminosity and magnetism extends outwards to a distance more or less identical with the length of the outstretched arm. And it is within this aura, as we call it, that the physical man exists rather like a kernel within a nut. Circulating the force admitted into the system by the former mental exercises is tantamount to charging it to a considerable degree in every department of its nature with life and energy. Naturally this is bound to exert a considerable influence, so far as general health is concerned, upon the enclosed 'kernel' within.

The final method of circulation rather resembles the action of a fountain. Just as water is forced or drawn up through a pipe until it jets up above, falling in a spray on all sides, so does the power directed by this last circulation. Throw the mind downwards to the Earth centre, imagining it to be the culmination of all the others, the receptacle of all power, the storehouse and terminal of the incoming vital force. Then imagine that this power ascends, or is drawn or sucked upwards by the magnetic attraction of the Spirit centre above the crown of the head. The power ascends the shaft and then falls down within the confines of the ovoid aura. When it has descended to the feet it is again gathered together and concentrated in the Earth centre preparatory to being pushed up the shaft again. As before, the fountain circulation should accompany a definite rhythm of inhalation and exhalation. By these means, the healing force is distributed to every part of the body. No single atom or cell in any organ or limb is omitted from the influence of its healing regenerative power.

The circulation completed, the mind may be permitted to dwell on the idea of the sphere of light, spiritual and healing in quality, surrounding the entire body. The visualization should be made as vivid and as powerful as possible. The sensation, following the partial or complete formulation of the aura in the manner described, is so marked and definite as to be quite unmistakable. In the first place it is marked by an extreme sense of calmness and vitality and poise, as though the mind was placid and still. The body, completely at rest in a state of relaxation, feels in all its parts thoroughly charged and permeated by the vibrant current of life. The skin over all the body will throw up symptoms, caused by the intensification of life within, of a gentle pricking and warmth. The eyes become clear and bright, the skin takes on a fresh healthy glow, and every faculty, mental, emotional and physical, becomes enhanced to a considerable degree.

Focusing Energy

This is the moment when, should there be any functional disturbances in any organ or limb, the attention should be directed and focused on that part. The result of this focus of attention directs a flow of energy over and above the general equilibrium just established. The diseased organ becomes bathed in a sea of light and power. Diseased tissue and diseased cells, under the stimulus of such power, become gradually broken down and ejected from the personal sphere. The revitalized blood-stream is then able to send to that spot new nourishment and new life so that new tissue, fibre, cells, etc., can easily be built up. In this way, health is restored by the persistent concentration there of the divine power. Carried on for a few days in the case of superficial ailments, and for months in the event of chronic and severe troubles, all symptoms may successfully be banished without others coming to take their place. There is no suppression of symptoms. Elimination is the result of these methods. Even psychogenic erruptions may thus be cured. For the currents of force arise from the deepest strata of the unconscious, where these psychoneuroses have their origin and where they lock up the nervous energy, preventing spontaneous and free expression of the psyche. The upwelling of the libido, as the vital force is called in psychological circles, dissolves the crystallizations and armoured barriers which divide the various strata of psychic function.

Where organic disease is the problem to be attacked, the procedure to be followed is slightly different. (One should still be under the care of a competent physician.) In this instance a considerably stronger current of force is required such as will dissolve the lesion and be sufficient to set in motion those systemic and metabolic activities to construct new tissue and cellular structure. To fulfil these conditions in an ideal sense a second person may be requisite so that his vitality added to that of the sufferer may overcome the condition. A useful technique which my experience has discovered supremely successful, and which any student can adopt, is first of all to relax completely every tissue throughout the body before attempting the Middle Pillar technique. The patient is placed in a highly relaxed state, one in which every neuromuscular tension has been tested and called to the attention of the patient. Consciousness is then able to eliminate tension and induce a relaxed state of that muscle or limb. I have found a useful preliminary in the practice of spinal manipulation and massage, with deep kneadings and effleurage, for in this way an enhanced circulation of the blood and lymph is produced – which from the physiological point of view is half the battle won. A suitable degree of relaxation obtained, the patient's feet are crossed over the ankles and his finger interlaced to rest lightly over the solar plexus. The operator or healer then seats himself on the right side of the person should the patient be right-handed – vice versa for a left-handed patient. Placing his right hand gently on the solar plexus under the patient's intertwined hands, and his left hand on the patient's head, at once a form of *rapport* is established. Within a few minutes a free circulation of magnetism and vitality is set up, readily discernible both by patient and healer.

The patient's attitude should be one of absolute receptivity to the incoming force – automatic, should he have unwavering confidence and faith in the operator's integrity and ability. Silence and quiet should be maintained for a short while, following which the operator silently performs the practice of the Middle Pillar, still maintaining his physical contact with the patient. His awakened spiritual centres act on the patient by sympathy. A similar awakening is introduced with the patient's sphere, and his centres eventually begin to operate and throw an equilibrated stream of energy into his system. Even when the operator does not vibrate the divine names audibly, the power flowing through his fingers sets up an activity which will surely produce some degree of healing activity within the patient. His psycho-spiritual centres are sympathetically stirred into the active assimilation and projection of force so that, without any conscious effort on his part, his sphere is invaded by the divine power of healing and life.

When the operator arrives at the circulation stage, he so employs his inner visualizing faculty, a veritable magical power indeed, that the augmented currents of energy flow not only through his own sphere but through that of his patient as well. The nature of this *rapport* now begins to undergo a subtle change. Whereas formerly there existed close sympathy and a harmonious frame of mind, mutually held, during and after the circulation there is an actual union and interblending of the two energy fields. They unite to form a single continuous sphere as the interchange and transference of vital energy proceed. Thus the operator, or his unconscious psyche or spiritual self, is able to divine exactly what potential his projected current should be, and precisely to where it should be directed.

A number of these treatments incorporating the cooperation and training of the patient in the use of mental methods should certainly go far in alleviating the original condition. Occasionally, since fanaticism above all is to be eschewed, medical and manipulative methods may usefully be combined with the mental methods described to facilitate and hasten the cure.

Although I have stressed healing of physical ills in the above, it cannot be insisted upon too strongly that this method is suitable for application to a host of other problems. This description of technique will be found adequate for all other situations which may come before

the student – whether it be a problem of poverty, character development, social or marital difficulties – and in fact any other problem type
of which one can think.

Recapitulation: The Preliminaries

Repetition is often invaluable both in teaching and in learning new
subjects. Hence some recapitulation of the various processes involved
in the Middle Pillar practice will help to clarify some of the issues. And
I should like to add a further consideration which will help to render
the entire method more effectual, lifting it to a higher plane of spiritual
understanding and achievement. This final step will enable the student
to call into operation dynamic factors within the human psyche which
will aid in the production of the desired result.

The first step, as we have seen, is a psycho-physical exercise. The
student must learn how to relax, how to loosen the chronic grip of
neuromuscular tensions in his body. Every involuntary tension in any
group of muscles or tissues in any area of the body must be brought
within the scope of his conscious awareness. Awareness is the magical
key by means of which such tension may literally be melted away and
dissolved. Only a little practice is necessary for this, and skill is very
readily obtained. The important conclusion following upon physical
relaxation is that the mind itself in all its departments and
ramifications undergoes a similar relaxation.

Psychic tension and somatic inflexibility are the great barriers to
realizing the omnipresence of the body of God. They actually prevent
one from becoming aware of the ever-presence of the life-force, the
dependence of the mind upon – even its ultimate identity with – the
Universal Mind, the Collective Unconscious. The mind's petty
barriers eliminated, and life flowing through its extensive organization,
almost immediately we become conscious of the dynamic principle
pervading and permeating all things. This step is without question the
all-important phase in the application of these psycho-spiritual
techniques.

Once having become aware of the preceding, the logical procedure
is to awaken the inner spiritual centres which can handle, as it were,
this high-voltage power and transform it into a usable human quality.
Possibly the easiest way to conceive of this is to liken the spiritual part
of man to a radio receiving set. The instrument must first be started
with power either from the battery or from the main before it will
work. Once power is flowing through it, then the rest of the intricate
mechanism of wiring, transformers, condensers, tubes and antennae
are able to come into operation. So also with man. We can tune
ourselves to the Infinite more readily through the mechanism of

lighting up the inner centres, man's own radio tubes. When the radio set is operative, then the divine current can be shot through the set in various ways, until both body and mind become powerfully vitalized and strong with spiritual energy.

Prayer

But all this is merely preparatory. The radio set may be lighted, the condensers and transformers and antennae in perfect operation – but what do we want to do with it? So also here. We need money. Sickness is present. Or we have undesirable moral or mental traits – or what not. We have so to elevate our minds, in the utilization of this spiritual energy, that the desire of our heart automatically realizes itself with practically no effort at all. The wish, the heart's desire, the goal to be reached, must be held firmly in mind, vitalized by divine power, but propelled forward into the universe by the fiery intensity of all the emotional exaltation we are capable of. Prayer is therefore indispensable. Prayer, not merely as a petition to some God outside the universe, but prayer conceived as the spiritual and emotional stimulus calculated to bring about an identification with or realization of our own Godhead, Prayer, sincerely undertaken, will mobilize all the qualities of the self, and the inner fervour that it will awaken will reinforce the work previously done. It will render success an almost infallible result. For in such a case, success comes not because of one's own human effort, but because God brings about the result. The fervour and the emotional exaltation enable one to realize the divinity within, which is the spiritual factor which brings our desires to immediate and complete fulfilment.

But I question whether prayer of the quiet unemotional variety has any value at all here. This cold-blooded petitioning finds no place within the highest conceptions of spiritual achievement. An ancient metaphysician once said, 'Inflame thyself with prayer.' Here is the secret. We must so pray that the whole of our being becomes aflame with a spiritual intensity before which nothing can stand. All illusions and all limitations fade away utterly before this fervour. When the soul literally burns up, then spiritual identity with God is attained. Then the heart's desire is accomplished without effort – because God does it. The wish becomes fact – objective, phenomenal fact, for all to see.

What prayers, then, should be employed to lift the mind to this intensity, to awaken the emotional fervour of which it was said 'inflame thyself in praying'? That I conceive to be a problem to be solved each one for himself. Every man and woman has some idea about prayer which, when sustained, will inflame him to inward realization. Some people will use a poem that has always had the effect of exalting them. Others will use the Lord's prayer, or maybe Psalm 23. And so on for all possible types. For myself, I prefer the use of some archaic hymns known as invocations, but which are prayers nonetheless, which certainly have the desired effect upon me of arousing the necessary emotional potential. In the hope that these might be useful to others, I append herewith a couple of fragments, the first one being composed of versicles from various scriptures.

I am the Resurrection and the Life. Whosoever believeth on me though he were dead, yet shall he live, and whosoever liveth and believeth on me shall have everlasting life. I am the First, and I am the Last. I am He that liveth and was dead – but behold! I am alive for evermore, and hold the keys of hell and death. For I know that my Redeemer liveth and that he shall stand at the latter day upon the Earth. I am the Way, the Truth, and the Life. No man cometh unto the Father but by me. I am the Purified. I have passed through the gates of darkness unto Light. I have fought upon earth for good. I have finished my work. I have entered into the invisible.

I am the Sun in his rising, passed through the hour of cloud and of night. I am Amoun, the Concealed One, the opener of the day. I am Osiris Onnophris, the Justified One, the Lord of Life, triumphant over death. There is no part of me which is *not* of the Gods. I am the Preparer of the Pathway, the Rescuer unto the Light. Let the White Light of the Divine Spirit Descend.

The second fragment is rather different from the above although both have a similar personal effect when slowly repeated, meditated upon, and felt intensely. This second prayer consists of two parts – the first one being a sort of petition of the higher divine self, whilst the second part bespeaks of the realization of identity with it.

Thee I invoke the Bornless One. Thee that didst create the Earth and the Heavens. Thee that didst create the Night and Day. Thee that didst create the Darkness and the Light. Thou art Man-Made-Perfect, whom no man hath seen at any time. Thou art God and very God. Thou has distinguished between the Just and the Unjust. Thou didst make the female and the male. Thou didst produce the seed and the fruit. Thou didst form men to love one another and to hate one another. Thou didst produce the moist and the dry, and That which nourisheth all created things.

The second half should follow only after a long pause, in which one attempts to realize just what it is that the prayer has asserted, and that it is raising the mind to an appreciation of the hidden secret Godhead within, which is the creator of all things.

This is the Lord of the Gods. This is the Lord of the Universe. This is He whom the winds fear. This is He, who having made voice by his commandment is Lord of all things, king, ruler and helper. Hear me and make all spirits subject unto me, so that every spirit of the firmament and of the ether, upon the earth and under the earth, on dry land and in the water, of whirling air, and of rushing fire, and every spell and scourge of God the Vast One may be made obedient unto me.

I am He, the Bornless Spirit, having sight in the feet, strong and the immortal Fire. I am He, the Truth, I am He who hate that evil should be wrought in the world. I am He that lighteneth and thundereth. I am He from whom is the shower of the Life of Earth. I am He whose mouth ever flameth. I am He, the begetter and manifester unto the Light. I am He, the Grace of the World. The Heart Girt with a Serpent is my Name.

These prayer fragments are suggested only and are to be used or rejected, as each student feels fit. They operate for me — they may operate in the case of other students, or not, as the case may be.

Non-therapeutic Uses

Quite apart from therapy, there are other uses of the Middle Pillar technique as I have intimated above. The enterprising student will divine his own usages for it.

It may be for various reasons that certain necessities of life, either physical or spiritual, have been denied one — with a consequent cramping effect on character and the onset of a sense of frustration. The latter always has a depressing and inhibitory effect on the human mind, producing indecision, inefficiency and inferiority. There is no real necessity why there should be any undue frustration and inhibition in our lives. A certain amount is no doubt inevitable. So long as we remain human it is quite certain that in some measure we are likely to be thwarted in our efforts fully to express the inner self, thus experiencing some degree of frustration. But any abnormal measure or persistent sense of thwarting and frustration may be dealt with and, by these mental and spiritual methods, eliminated.

First of all an understanding of life is essential, and an unconditional acceptance of everything in life and every experience that may come one's way. With understanding will come a love of life and living, for love and understanding are one and the same. It will also foster the determination no longer to frustrate natural processes but by acceptance to cooperate with nature. The methods of spiritual

and mental culture have long held out hope that these inhibitory
conditions may be alleviated.

Poverty of estate as well as of idea is a life-condition which these
techniques have always acknowledged to be amenable to treatment.
The usual method is one of such deep and prolonged reflection upon
just that mental stimulus, moral quality or material thing which is
wanted, that the idea of the need sinks into the so-called subconscious
mind. If the barriers leading to the subconscious are penetrated so that
the latter accepts the idea of the need, then, so it is said, sooner or later
life will inevitably attract one of those things required. But, as with all
therapeutic methods, there were so many instances where, despite
close adherence to the prescribed techniques, success was not
forthcoming. It is my contention, therefore, that they fail for very
much the same reasons that their healing efforts fail. In short, it was
because there was no true understanding of the interior
psychodynamic mechanism whereby such effects could be produced.
There was no appreciation of the methods by which the dynamic
nature of the unconscious could so be stimulated that the human
personality became transformed into a powerful magnet attracting to
itself whatever it truly desired or was necessary to its welfare.

Whether this procedure is morally defensible is a question I do not
wish to discuss at length, though I know it will be raised. But the
answer is brief. Whatever faculties we have are meant to be used, and
used both for our own advantage and that of others. If we are in a
state of constant mental friction, emotional frustration, and excessive
poverty, I fail to see in what way we can be of service either to
ourselves or our fellow men. Eliminate these restrictions first, improve
the mental and emotional faculties so that the spiritual nature is able
to penetrate through the personality and manifest itself in practical
ways, then we are in a position to be of some service to those with
whom we come into contact. The preliminary stimulation of the
psycho-spiritual centres within, and then formulating clearly and
vividly one's demands upon the universe is capable of attracting
almost anything required, so long, naturally, as it exists within the
bounds of reason and possibility.

Using the Astrological Structure

First of all, let me preface my further remarks by stating that from the
practical point of view the rudiments of the astrological schema are of
untold value in that they offer a concise classification of the broad
divisions of things. I am not concerned here with astrology as such,
merely that it is convenient to use its schema. Its roots are in the seven
principal ideas or planets to which most ideas and things may be

referred. To each of these root ideas there is attributed a positive and negative colour, and a divine name for the purpose of vibration. I propose naming the planets with their principal attributions as follows:

Saturn. Older people and old plans. Debts and their repayment. Agriculture, real estate, death, wills, stability, inertia. Positive colour indigo; negative black. *Jehovah Elo-him*, pronounced *Yeh-hoh-voh Eh-loh-heem.*

Jupiter. Abundance, plenty, growth, expansion, generosity. Spirituality, visions, dreams, long journeys. Bankers, creditors, debtors, gambling. Positive colour purple; negative blue. *El*, pronounced exactly as written.

Mars. Energy, haste, anger, construction or destruction (according to application), danger, surgery. Vitality and magnetism. Will-power. Positive and negative colours bright red. *Elohim Gibor*, pronounced *Eh-loh-heem Gibor.*

Sun. Superiors, employers, executives, officials. Power and success. Life, money, growth of all kinds. Illumination, imagination, mental power. Health. Positive colour orange; negative colour yellow or gold. *Jehovah Eloah ve-Daas*, pronounced *Yeh-hoh-voh El-loh-ve-dah-ahs*, IAO, as explained previously.

Venus. Social affairs, affections and emotions, women, younger people. All pleasures and the arts, music, beauty, extravagance, luxury, self-indulgence. Both colours emerald green. *Jehovah Tzavoös*, pronounced *Yeh-hoh-voh Tsah-voh-ohs.*

Mercury. Business matters, writing, contracts, judgement and short travels. Buying, selling, bargaining. Neighbours, giving and obtaining information. Literary capabilities, and intellectual friends. Books, papers. Positive colour yellow; negative colour orange. *Elohim Tzavoös.*

Moon. General public, women. Sense-reactions. Short journeys and removals. Changes and fluctuations. The personality. Positive colour blue; negative colour puce. *Shah-dai El Chai.*

These very briefly are the attributions of the planets under which almost everything and every subject in nature may be classified. This classification is extremely useful because it simplifies enormously one's task of physical and spiritual development. It may be best if before concluding I instance a few simple and elementary examples to illustrate the function and method of employing these correspondences.

Using Astrological Correspondences

Suppose I am engaged in certain studies requiring books that are not easily obtainable from booksellers. Despite my every demand for them, in spite of widespread advertising and willingness to pay a reasonable price for them, my efforts are unavailing. The result is that for the time my studies are held up. This delay reaches the point when it is excessive and irritating, and I decide to use my own technical methods for ending it. At certain prescribed intervals, preferably upon awakening in the morning and before retiring to sleep at night, I practise the rhythmic breath and the Middle Pillar. By these methods I have made available enormous quantities of spiritual power, and transformed the unconscious into a powerful storage battery, ready to project or attract power to fulfil my need. This I circulate through the auric system.

My next step consists of visualizing the negative or passive colour of Mercury, orange, so that meditating upon it changes the surrounding auric colour to that hue. Orange is used because books, which I need, are attributed to Mercury; and I employ the negative colour because it tends to make the sphere of sensation open, passive and receptive. Then I proceed to charge and vitalize the sphere by vibrating the appropriate divine name again and again, until it seems to my perceptions that all the mercurial forces of the universe react to the magnetic attraction of that sphere. All the forces of the universe are imagined to converge upon my sphere, attracting to me just those books, documents, critics, friends and so on, needed to further my work. Inevitably, after persistent and concentrated work I hear from friends or booksellers quite by chance, so it would see, that these books are available. Introductions are procured to the right people, and taken by and large my work is assisted. The results occur, however, in a perfectly natural way.

One is not to imagine that the use of these methods contravenes the known laws of nature and that miraculous phenomena will occur. Far from it. There is nothing in them that is supernatural. These methods are based upon the use of psychic principles normally latent within man, and which everyone possesses. No individual is unique in this respect. And the use of these psychic principles brings results through quite normal but unsuspected channels.

On the other hand, should I desire to help a colleague who has literary aspirations but at a certain juncture finds his style cramped and the free flow of ideas inhibited, I should alter my method in one particular point only. Instead of using orange as before, I should visualize the aura as of a yellow or golden colour, though the vibratory name would be the same. Again, instead of imagining the universal forces to have a centripetal motion towards my sphere, I should attempt to realize that the mercurial forces awakened within me by the colour visualization and vibration are being projected from me to my patient. If he, too, becomes quiet and meditative at the same hour, my help becomes more powerful since he consciously assists my efforts with a similar meditation. But this need not be insisted upon. For, as shown by telepathy experiments, the greater part of the receiver's impressions are unconsciously received. Therefore, in the case of the patient, his own unconscious psyche will pick up automatically and of necessity the inspiration and power I have telepathically forwarded to him *in absentia.*

This system combines telepathic suggestion with the willed communication of vital power. I strenuously oppose those partitive apologists who uphold in theory the one faculty to the detriment of the other. Some deny suggestion or telepathy, and argue over-enthusiastically on behalf of vital magnetism. Others refuse categorically to admit the existence of magnetism, pressing their proofs exclusively in favour of telepathy and suggestion. Both, to my mind, are incorrect and dogmatic when insisting upon their idea alone as having universal validity or as being the sole logical mode of explanation. Equally, each is right in some respects and in a certain number of cases; there is a place for both in the natural economy of things. The resources of nature are both great and extensive enough to admit the mutual existence of both of them, and innumerable other powers also.

Self-analysis

The technical procedure is, as I have shown, extremely simple – even where employed for subjective ends. Suppose the realization suddenly comes to me that instead of being the magnanimous person I had imagined myself to be I am really mean and stingy. Of course I could go through a course of psychoanalysis to discover *why* my nature early in life had become warped so that a habit of meanness was engendered. But this is a lengthy and costly business – bad arguments, admittedly, against its necessity. And so much would depend upon the analyst and his relations with myself. Instead, however, I might resort to the following technique. My first steps consist of those described above – rhythmic breathing, the light-shaft formulated from head to foot, and the circulation of force through the aura. Then remembering that a generous outlook upon and an attitude towards life is a

Jupiterian quality, I would surround myself with an azure sphere whilst vibrating frequently and powerfully the divine name *El*. It depends entirely upon one's skill and familarity with the system whether the names are vibrated silently or audibly, but by either way, powerful Jupiterian currents would permeate my being. I would even visualize every cell being bathed in an ocean of blueness; and I would attempt to imagine currents invading my sphere from every direction, so that all my thinking and feeling is literally in terms of blueness. Slowly a subtle transformation ensues. That is, it would were I really sincere, desirous of correcting my faults, and if I did attempt to become generous enough as to perform the practice faithfully and often.

Likewise, if a friend or patient complained of a similar vice in him, appealing to me for help, in this instance I would use a positive colour for projection. I would formulate my sphere as an active dynamic purple sphere, rich and royal in colour, and project its generous, healing, and fecund influence upon his mind and personality. With time the fault would be corrected to his satisfaction and thus enhance his spiritual nature.

And so on, with everything else. These few examples will, I am sure, have shown the application of the methods.

It is not enough simply to wish for certain results and idly expect them to follow. Failure only can come from such an idle course. Anything worth while and likely to succeed requires a great deal of work and perseverance. The Middle Pillar technique is certainly no exception. But devotion to it is extremely worthwhile because of the nature and quality of the results which follow. Once a day will demonstrate the efficacy of the method. Twice a day would be much better – especially if there is some illness or psychic difficulty to overcome. After a while, the student who is sincere and in whom the spiritual nature is gradually unfolding, will apply himself to the method quite apart from the promise which I have here held out. Healing powers, freedom from poverty and worry, happiness – all these are eminently desirable. But over and above all of these is the desirability of knowing and expressing the spiritual self within – though it may be in some cases that this ideal is hardly attainable until some measure of fulfilment in other respects and on other levels has been achieved. When, however, the ideal is realized as desirable, then the value of this method will also be realized as supremely effectual to that end.